HOW TO DESIGN
BRAIN-FRIENDLY
FLEXIBLE OFFICES

Based on science, not on opinions
Theo Compernolle

Compublications

Readers' comments about BrainChains

Stunning work, aggregating the best and newest research to create a User Manual for Your Brain! Whether all the new tech is leveraged as a positive tool or allowed to seduce us into numb- and dumbness is a fine line, and Theo delineates that with brilliance. Read at your peril.

David Allen

Excellent book on productivity. If you have read David Allen's Getting Things Done this book will be beneficial to comprehend the whole system and why we do what we do. Theo Compernolle's work is based on scientific research and backs up his arguments in style. If there is one thing you should take from BrainChains "Do not use your phone while driving" :-)

Addo General Mrch

I'm so glad I got my hands on this book. Forget all the other business books, tips and theories which everybody else uses, THIS is the book that will separate you away from the herd and should be read before anything else. This book will be kept on my desk instead of my bookshelf, as a constant reminder.

NoName

In a few words: an amazing book. Loved reading it. The author knows very well how to explain this matter in an open end very comprehensible way. I look at my laptop in a different way now. Must read!

4bozzza

This is one of those books that do have impact on your habits ... at least for me it did and that is I think the biggest value a book can have...

Joanne

... an easy to read "page turner"... which I feel everyone in the "connected" world should read.

Dave Scott, President

Top experience. Extended documentation.Accessible reading of "scientific" topics. Really professional. Appreciate the style and art of communication of the author. Congratulations. Excellent buy and investment.

Jean-Paul Antonus

"... a compelling, meticulously researched, and cleverly illustrated case against the twin tyrannies of hyperconnectivity and multitasking... also shows how to free ourselves from them"

Nélida and Jorge Colapinto

It is amazing (and disturbing) that what Theo writes of is so little known and/or poorly embraced by the business world. ... Yet the working practices encouraged by firms, and societies as a whole serve to squander our IQ, EQ and SQ and foster burnout, unrealised potential and underperformance.....And the hyperconnectivity of recent years brought about by the smartphone has magnified the problem multiple-fold. Congratulations to Theo for bringing this issue into the open with such a well-evidenced, thoughtful and readable analysis.

L. Watson

HOW TO DESIGN BRAIN-FRIENDLY FLEXIBLE OFFICES

Prof Dr Theo Compernolle
Compublications 2018

ISBN 978-90-822058-9-3

CONTACT: office@compernolle.com

ILLUSTRATIONS: Huw Aaron. contact@huwaaron.com

DESIGN: Ivan Stojic stojagrozny@gmail.com

Information about BrainChains: www.brainchains.info

Available at www.amazon.com
For 5 copies or more, you can also contact
office@compernolle.com

"The cages in modern zoos are better for animals, than modern offices for people...

because modern ZOO-directors know more about the inborn needs of their animals, than company-directors about the innate needs of people... "

Theo Compernolle. 2014

"Noise is the most impertinent of all forms of interruption. It is not only an interruption, but also a disruption of thought. Of course, where there is nothing to interrupt, noise will not be so particularly painful."

Arthur Schopenhauer: On Noise. 1851

"The most negative influence on my intellectual productivity is my office."

Countless professionals

"An office shared with more than three people, is a good place to work."

Only 13% *of 1100 professionals half of them managers*

Contents

FOREWORD OF THE 2018 EDITION: Designing a good brain-friendly office is a daunting challenge.

When a company hires modern brainworkers the goal is that they study, understand and communicate complex and often difficult subjects to deliver high quality work, novel ideas and solutions in a sustainable way. To do this, sustained, uninterrupted focus is critical. Their offices therefore should first of all be places that not just allow but encourage focus and secondly enhance communication.

The task of executives planning an office is very important, complex and difficult. Matthew Davis summarizes it as following[1]:

> *"The design and operation of workspace has always been driven by a number of often competing interests, such as:*
>
> **1.** *The cost of building, maintaining and servicing the space;*
>
> **2.** *Providing for the comfort and security of occupants;*
>
> **3.** *Accommodating new technologies;*
>
> **4.** *Supporting working styles and processes;*
>
> **5.** *Upholding organizational structure and corporate image;*
>
> **6.** *Aiding recruitment (through providing an attractive place to work);*
>
> **7.** *Location*
>
> **8.** *Changing economic circumstances*
>
> **9.** *Change of the nature of work itself "*

A fundamental mistake is to consider the building or leasing of an office as a real-estate project. It's absolutely not.

The impact of a new office on the company and its culture is so big, deep and broad that it should be tackled as an important strategic change project.

I have the impression that many executives (and architects) avoid this daunting task, hard study and responsibility with safe lemming behavior: "If a successful company like Facebook or X (fill in your choice) does it, it certainly will be OK". It's not OK at all.

Other executives avoid the hard work by leasing offices from real estate companies whose business model is to build the cheapest possible offices and to lease them out with the biggest possible margins. They do not care about the productivity and wellbeing of the office workers.

The result is that 70% of the offices are badly designed Open Plan Offices.

Recent research about these open offices, confirms the conclusions of the first (2014) and second (2017) edition of this book and adds new elements.

Open offices have advantages

- Above all they are cheaper, which often is the main reason they are built or rented.

- They are flexible to adapt to the rise and fall of the number of employees present

- They are loved by people who never had the experience of the tremendous power and joy of persistent, uninterrupted concentration

- They stimulate people to be busy.

Open offices have disadvantages

- First of all they have a very negative impact on intellectual productivity, creativity, motivation, satisfaction, stress and status-anxiety, trust, cooperation and wellbeing of a big majority.

- The order of negative impact is: 1. Hot-desking 2. Open plan 3. Flex office 3. Cubicle 4. Private

- Contrary to the popular management myth, they do not improve real communication nor collaboration, on the contrary!

- They are unhealthier: people get ill more often

- They interrupt people's attention every two minutes.

- They have a negative impact on supervisor support.

- They stimulate people to look busy: constant inefficient and ineffective busyness, which is not good for business.

- They are noisy: especially conversations and above all phone conversations continuously disrupt the concentration.

- Their negative impact is highest on employees who have had the experience of accomplishing much more and better in an environment that allowed them to concentrate

- Introverts who love to delve deep into their work suffer more.

- They have a special negative impact on the work of women, they experience more sexism, especially in a macho environment.

- They are penny-wise but very pound-foolish: they are a waste of money in the middle and long term. For every 1,-€ you save with an open office you lose 5,-€.

Conclusion: most open offices are a waste of minds and money.

This is not just my opinion, which you can counter with your opinion. These are the conclusions of hundreds of research publications. They make the difference between an opinion and an informed opinion. Ignore them at your peril.

FOREWORD OF THE 2017 EDITION:
The Open Office Is Naked

Once upon a time there was an emperor whose only interest in life was to dress up in fashionable clothes. He kept changing his clothes so that people could admire him.

Two swindlers disguised themselves as top class tailors and promised him the finest, best suit of clothes from a fabric so light and fine that it would seem invisible to anyone who was unfit for his position or "hopelessly stupid".

The emperor was very excited and ordered the new tailors to begin their work.

One day, the king asked the prime minister to go and see how much work the two tailors had done. He saw the two men moving scissors in the air but he could see no cloth! He kept quiet for fear of being called stupid and unfit for his job. Instead, he praised the fabric and said it was marvelous.

Finally, the emperor's new dress was ready. The "tailors" mimed dressing him He could see nothing but he too did not want to appear stupid or unfit for his position.

He admired the dress and thanked the tailors. He was asked to parade down the street for all to see the new clothes.

The emperor paraded down the main street. The townsfolk could only see a naked emperor but played along with the pretense for fear of being thought stupid or unfit for their jobs.

They foolishly praised the invisible fabric and the colors and the emperor was very happy.

At last, a child in the crowd, too young to understand the desirability of keeping up the pretense, shouted out loud: "The emperor is naked!"

Soon everyone began to murmur the same thing and very soon all shouted, "The emperor is naked!"

The emperor cringed, suspected the assertion was true, but walked on proudly, preferring to believe that his people were stupid.[2]

To understand why the open office is naked, why it is so bad for brainwork, you should know a few things about your thinking brain.

FOREWORD OF THE 2014 EDITION:
Senior Executives, Please Beware.

I know that what I write in this booklet is not going to be well received by some of my most important clients: senior executives and CEO's. Sometimes in this text, I can't hide my anger, disappointment or sadness when I see how executives, due to a lack of knowledge, spoil the quality of the work and the wellbeing of so many employees. You may even experience this book as pedantic, paternalistic and disrespectful. However, I am always very transparent, frank and direct with my clients, because I think that is the best way to inspire and help them. Since I am an independent scholar I am free to talk straight, very straight.

Given the success of "BRAINCHAINS"[1] I am all the time invited by organizations for workshops and presentations about these "BrainChains", but then, too often I am kindly requested not to talk about the negative impact of open offices. I do not comply. If participants ask questions about the open office, I give them the facts. There often are already too many people inside and outside organisations who adapt and alter the facts to fit the opinion of the CEO and the executives.

I learned in the past five years that many business leaders choose to ignore the feedback from their employees as well as the hard scientific evidence, even if this attitude undermines the long term productivity and wellbeing of their employees. I hope this is just a lack of knowledge and that reading the facts will inspire them to tackle the issue differently

> *"Because modern ZOO-directors know more about the inborn needs of their animals, than company-directors about the innate needs of*

---

1 see **www.brainchains.info**

people ... the cages in modern zoos are better for animals, than modern offices for people."

When I discover in my research that a great many offices significantly reduce the intellectual productivity and wellbeing of employees, I share this with you, even if you don't like the idea that your decisions about office design are not optimal, just plain wrong or demonstrating a lack of knowledge. What's more, this booklet is not just my personal opinion; I am summarizing shiploads of research and giving my conclusions.

You're a knowledge worker. But what do you really know about your most important instrument, your brain? For 99% of the professionals the answer is: NOTHING and a few urban myths. What do you know about the effect on your brain, your intellectual productivity and wellbeing, of the improper use of the wonderful information and communication technology, to always be online, multi-tasking, constant stress, lack of sleep and ... poorly designed open offices?

You may happen to have a personal opinion, an opinion that in your function has daily impact on thousands of people for better or worse, but on what is it based?

> *"You are not entitled to your opinion. You are entitled to your informed opinion. No one is entitled to be ignorant."*

Harlan Ellison

On the other hand, if you are receptive to this knowledge, you will learn a lot that's useful and very lucrative for you and your business and for the wellbeing of your employees. This is especially true if you integrate your thinking about your offices with longer term strategic choices about the desired company culture, productivity, collaboration, resilience, mobility and flexibility of your workforce. Moreover your offices are part of your marketing image not only towards your clients but also in your fight for talent.

Theo Compernolle
July 2014

About the author

Prof Dr Theo Compernolle MD. PhD. Is an adjunct professor at the CEDEP European Centre for Executive Development. He teaches and coaches in the executive programs of business schools in several countries.

He also consults, teaches and coaches professionals, managers and executives in a wide range of (multi)national companies, professional services firms and training institutions in many different cultures and countries.

He holds these sessions in English, Dutch and French.

He has held the positions of Suez Chair in Leadership and Personal Development at the Solvay Business School, Adjunct Professor at INSEAD, visiting professor at several business schools and Professor at the Free University of Amsterdam.

As a medical doctor, neuropsychiatrist, psychotherapist and business consultant, Theo studies research from very different fields including medicine, biology, psychology, neurology, physiology and management. He then burns the midnight oil to integrate this information into a coherent whole and to find simple ways to pass on this knowledge, in a memorable way, to all kinds of professionals. His clients often call his sessions "Science made simple and useful".

Theo was first drawn into the world of business after the publication of his PhD about stress caused quite a stir in the media.

Since then he has become an expert on the emotional and relational aspects of leadership and enhancing the resilience of executives, executive teams, organizations and families with a business, especially in times of conflict, stress and change.

He has published several non-fiction books and more than a hundred scientific articles. Three of his books ao. "STRESS: FRIEND AND FOE. Vital Stress Management at work and in the family" became bestsellers and long-sellers.

His most recent book "BRAINCHAINS. Discover your brain and unleash its full potential in a hyperconnected multitasking world" received 4-5-star reviews on Amazon. com. It is published in Russian and Chinese. The Dutch translation was on the top-10 best-sellers list.

For people lacking the time to read comprehensive books, he wrote a concise version of 50 pages of 250 words, 1 subject per page, with 50 illustrations. It is published in English, French and Dutch. An e-learning program (adapted for smartphone) is available in Dutch.

More information at: **www.brainchains.info**

He has also been a manager himself as the director of several inpatient and outpatient departments.

Theo gained a Ph.D. on his research into stress from the University of Amsterdam (the Netherlands). He is certified as a psychotherapist and as medical specialist in neuropsychiatry and psychotherapy. He trained at the universities of Amsterdam (The Netherlands), Leiden (The Netherlands) and Pennsylvania (USA) where he was a fellow. He graduated as a Medical Doctor from the Catholic University of Leuven (Belgium).

More information at **www.compernolle.com**

Contact: **office@compernolle.com**

THE FIFTH BRAINCHAIN: Open Offices
Why the fifth?

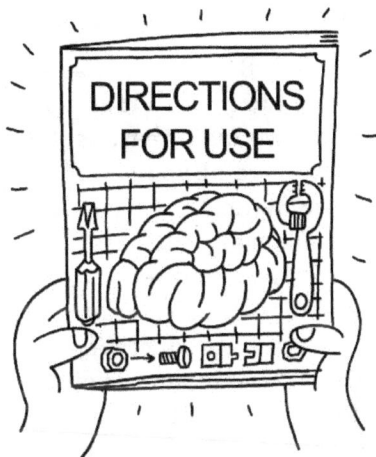

"The Fifth BrainChain" is an idea that developed as I was researching my book "BrainChains". This is a book for professionals to improve their intellectual productivity, which is the top contributor to economic growth and the top contributor to individual careers. It's a book how we can avoid ruining our intellectual abilities by chaining them with the BrainChains I briefly summarize in the next paragraph.

However, in every single presentation or workshop I gave about the original four BrainChains, participants reacted with *"Yes that may all be very true and useful, but for me, the most negative influence on my intellectual productivity is my awful open office"*.

This encouraged me to broaden my research and to find out if this was just a personal problem for a few or a generic problem. These people proved to be right: far too many offices make good brainwork basically impossible or so difficult that people are exhausted by the end of the day.

In fact badly designed offices lower our intellectual productivity by up to 30-50%. And so the Fifth Brain-Chain was born: brain hostile open offices.

For a while, the Fifth BrainChain was a chapter in my book. Then I decided to publish it as a separate booklet instead. Why? For two main reasons. Firstly, I wanted my book to focus on BrainChains that are within every-body's sphere of influence, things you can do yourself to improve your intellectual productivity. Your office does not fall into this category. In reality, unless you are an executive, there is not much you can do about an office design that undermines productivity, except trying to influence the top of your organization to do something about it or to join together with colleagues to increase the pressure. Secondly, I wanted the information about the Fifth BrainChain to be as freely available and as easy to distribute as possible.

The other FOUR BRAINCHAINS in a nutshell

BrainChains that ruin our intellectual productivity

To get the best out of our brain, we need to know some of the basics about how it works. If we then apply this knowledge to our daily work, we can significantly increase our intellectual productivity.

I prefer to speak about brainwork and brainworkers because "knowledge workers" are usually defined as "workers whose main capital is knowledge" and who "think for a living". Typical examples may include software engineers, architects, engineers, scientists and lawyers"[3].

I think this definition is too narrow and refers too much to an elite group of brainworkers.

My starting point is that today we are all brainworkers. Nurses, teachers, policemen, office workers and shop floor operators all earn their living first and foremost by using their knowledge, using their brain.

Routine manual work and simple cognitive work has been taken over by machines, robots and computers. The only work left is that which needs a human thinking-brain and social skills to connect your brain to that of others.

> *"In the developed world, all work needs a human thinking-brain and social skills to connect your brain to that of others."*

My conclusion, after screening more than 600 research articles and studying more than 400, is that we all unknowingly mess up our intellectual productivity more than we should. It is so bad that halfway through my research, I used the working title "How we unknowingly f*** up our brainwork".

I summarized my findings into four areas that undermine productivity and called them BrainChains because they prevent our thinking brain from soaring. While doing this research I also discovered that I undermined my own brainwork in ways that I had not previously realized!

Three brains influence our thinking and doing

Thinking Brain
Abstract thinking ex. LANGUAGE ! *Past, Present, Future, Phantasy*
One thing at a time !!
GOAL oriented

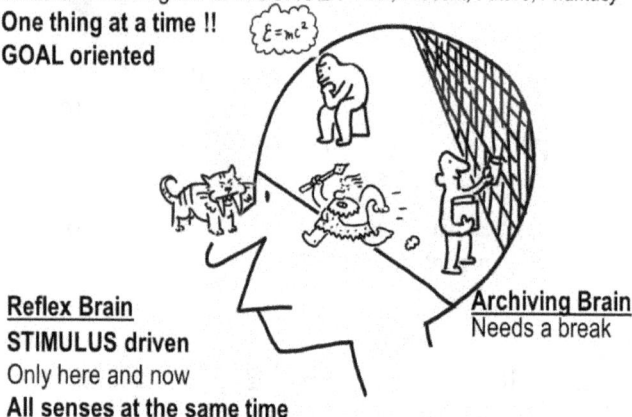

$$E = mc^2$$

Reflex Brain
STIMULUS driven
Only here and now
All senses at the same time

Archiving Brain
Needs a break

We should break these chains because of the direct negative impact they have on our intellectual productivity. We should also learn how to manage them better because they give our fast primitive reflex brain an unfair advantage over our slow, sophisticated thinking-brain and our archiving brain.

The role of these three brain systems is explained in the first section of "BrainChains" because first of all I want the reader to really understand the way our brain works.

In the second section I explain how we are constantly working against rather than with our brains so that readers can creatively invent their own solutions.

Only then, in the third section, do I present solutions, which are not there to be followed blindly but to act as a source of inspiration. I present examples at three levels, Me, We and They: what you can do without much help from others to improve your intellectual productivity; what you can do if you collaborate with others; and what they - the higher levels of your organization - should do

The first BrainChain and the root problem is "always being connected"

The problem (by problem I mean a real problem that you have to solve, not just a challenge that you can avoid), the root problem turns out to be "always being connected", sometimes referred to as hyperconnectivity. This leads to constantly trying to multitask, a continuous (low level of) stress and not enough sleep. These issues ruin our intellectual productivity.

> *"The opportunity to be always connected anytime, anywhere with anybody or any database is fantastic for our brain-work. However, always being connected is a disaster for our brainwork."*

When we are always connected we are in a reactive, ad-hoc mode that favours our ultra-fast but very primitive stimulus-driven reflex brain to the detriment of our slower but sophisticated goal-oriented thinking-brain.

This reflex-brain is stimulus driven; its so called "bottom-up attention" is caught by anything that is potentially dangerous, novel or fun. It functions 100% in the here and now. It only knows the world as far as it is within the reach of our senses. It cannot reflect on the past nor the future. When we do not control our reflex-brain, we become adhocrats (or adhoc-rats?) and our organizations adhocracies (or adhoc-crazies?).

Therefore, we need to better protect our most human, creative, yet very fragile and slow thinking-brain, from our fast, bestial reflex brain. Only our thinking-brain is goal-oriented, it can disconnect from the here and now, can do abstract thinking, can use experiences from the past and reflect on the future. Only our thinking-brain can be creative, wise and ethical. To do its work, it has to pay attention. This so called "top-down attention" consumes energy and willpower.

Always being connected also ruins real conversations with real people, and yet it is these conversations that are so crucial for developing deep knowledge and creative solutions.

Always being connected also causes information overload and prevents us from dealing with all that information more efficiently. The paradox is that we should regularly disconnect to reflect on our hyperconnectivity.

Always being connected also gets in the way of our archiving brain because even the smallest micro-breaks get filled with "work", usually doing emails and getting involved with antisocial media, and yet these breaks are so important for our archiving brain to order, reorder, store and retrieve information.

The solution is very simple: disconnect to reflect. Yet staying connected anytime and everywhere has for many people become a very bad habit that is not at all easy to undo. Busyness has replaced real work. For some of us it has even become an addiction in the psychiatric sense of the word. Fortunately there is a branch of scientific psychology that over the last 75 years has developed deep knowledge and practical tools to unlearn habits. We can use these to unchain our brain. To start with it will require a lot of willpower and discipline, but once you develop the new habit of not always being connected it will become much easier, and eventually second nature.

We should also let our brain idle regularly. "Brain breaks" are of utmost importance to give our archiving brain time not only to store the billions of bits of information but also to organize this information so that it can be retrieved and to help us to find the best and most creative solutions from all that stored information.

The second BrainChain is multitasking

Since our thinking-brain simply cannot multitask, it is useless and totally counter-productive to even try to do so, especially for tasks that require concentration, reflection or creativity. If you do multitask, it will take you at least four times as long to do a lousier job. It may even be a safety hazard.

The brutal fact is that our thinking brain cannot multitask. Period. There are two kinds of multitasking. 1. Simultaneous multitasking: trying to do two things at the same time like doing emails while having a phone conversation. 2. Serial multitasking: continuously jumping from one task to another, interrupting a task for another task

> *"The brutal fact is that our thinking brain cannot multitask. Trying to do it anyway is very ignorant or very stupid"*

What happens in fact when we try to multitask is that we switch from task to task and these switches are a big problem.

Task-switching is a huge and hugely underestimated source of errors, and waste of intellectual productivity. Each switch is a waste of time, waste of energy in its literal sense, waste of memory, waste of creativity, waste of accuracy, waste of quality and much more. On the shop floor these situations may create **safety hazards** that you had never thought of before.

Moreover, and of uttermost importance for the design of an office: every interruption is a switch. **Every interruption decreases the intellectual productivity in many ways.** Therefore, privacy in the sense of being protected against any unsolicited distracting or sensory interruptions, should be the first priority when designing an office. Contact should be the second. Further on I further explain this pseudo-dilemma and the solution of a flexible office with the right priorities.

On the level of the individual, the solution is to single-task, but for most of us this is not realistic. Therefore the best solution is to 'right-task', which basically means rigorous **batch-processing** ie. set aside time-limited slots during which you only deal with **one task, undisturbed.** First of all, for important thinking or conversations, we should allocate undisturbed time-slots, disconnect from the Internet and eliminate all possible distractions.

Einstein said: "It's not that I'm so smart; it's just that I stay with problems longer" and we should follow the example of Einstein and stay with our intellectual challenges for longer. If Einstein would have been glued to a smartphone and distracted all the time in a modern office, he would never have formulated his world-changing formula. If Steve Jobs would have worked in a modern office, glued to an iPhone, he would never have invented the iPhone.

> *"If Steve Jobs would have worked in an open office, glued to an iPhone, he would never have invented the iPhone!"*

This piece of advice may well be simple, but that doesn't mean it is easy to follow.

It is difficult enough for the modern brainworker to have the courage and discipline to disconnect to eliminate the major distractions within his control.

Why would companies want to make this even more difficult and ruin their intellectual productivity by warehousing them in brain-hostile offices?

Executives, managers, and especially Human Resources (HR) and Safety, Health and Environment (SHE) managers, should be on the lookout for situations where work is organized in such a way that it increases multitasking. They should provide a work environment where interruptions are eliminated as much as possible, because every interruption is a multitasking-switch, creating an ever growing black-hole of multitasking wherein productivity disappears without a trace.

The third BrainChain is negative stress

Always being connected creates stress. First because it puts you in a continuous alert-state. This does not necessarily cause high levels of stress, but chronic low levels of stress can be just as harmful and can further undermine your intellectual productivity.

Secondly, always being connected and multitasking make you so pathetically inefficient. The fact that you need much more time, work longer hours and that you make more mistakes will cause stress. Moreover, multitasking by itself costs more energy.

| Lack of Architectural Privacy | Lack of Perceived Privacy: NOISE! | Cognitive/Emotional Exhaustion |

The earliest victims of stress that is too much or lasts too long, are the most human, sophisticated competencies of your thinking-brain, such as abstract thinking, analysis, synthesis, abstraction, creativity, associative thinking and tangential thinking. Negative stress is a major reason why intelligent people do stupid things. If you are interested in the impact of stress on your body and brain, you can read more in my book "Stress: Friend and Foe".

One important aspect of good stress management is that the human being is built for stress; it is a perfect stress machine, but the stress it is built for is short stress.

To stay resilient we need regular breaks. Healthy stress is interval stress.

Hence the brain-breaks that our archiving brain needs in order to store and manipulate information are also very important for us to physically cope with stressful situations.

These breaks are also important to prevent chronic local stress that may result in pain in our thumbs, wrists, arms, neck, shoulders, back and head.

It is important to give some thought to the ergonomics of your workplace because once these body parts start hurting, and certainly once you develop Repetitive Strain Injury (RSI), this will seriously disturb your productivity and may be extremely difficult to cure.

Research, that I will discuss further-on, shows that brain-workers are to some extent able to concentrate in a badly designed noisy open office, but that this causes a measurable increase of chronic stress, even if they are not aware of it, and that they leave at the end of the day with more symptoms of exhaustion.

As I explain in "BrainChains", this tiredness at the end of the day results not only in worse work and worse decisions, but also in less ethical decision, and behaviour.

The fourth BrainChain is lack of pauses and sleep

Our archiving-brain that organizes and stores the billions of bits of information and that plays an important role in your creativity, does its work when our thinking brain takes a break. Therefore, regular breaks during a working day are important for your intellectual productivity. The most important break for your archiving brain is a good night of sleep. An remarkable amount of research points to the fact that having enough sleep is of utmost importance for your intellectual productivity in general and for your creativity in particular.

It is startling to discover how many professionals have become obsessed by "not losing time" and who fill their breaks with frenetically tapping their little screens. Having a break is an investment in your brainwork. Staying involved all the time with your screen is a real waste of time and energy.

Moreover, too many see even their sleep as "lost time" and deprive themselves of sleep and mess around with their biological clock, which greatly undermines the quality and quantity of their brainwork.

The solution is simple: get enough sleep, which for most of us is 7-8 hours. If you think you are the exception to this 7-8 hour rule, do the three tests in "BrainChains" to find out how much sleep your body and brain really need. You might belong to the 15% who really need less sleep, but there is a 70% chance that you are in for a surprise.

Email (and other messages) are a BrainChain that combines and reinforces the other four

Email is a great tool that has become a counterproductive time waster that undermines the intellectual productivity of far too many professionals and that even has a negative influence on the way our body functions. The worst way of dealing with emails and other messages is to check them all the time on a smartphone. This causes continuous unrelenting multi-tasking, ruining your intellectual efficiency, productivity and creativity.

You would expect that people in open offices communicate more and as a result email less. Interesting research, done with sophisticated sensors and checking of company email servers, showed that in reality the opposite happens: the more people in an open space, the less there is direct communication and the more people communicate with emails, even to people in the same space[4].

There is only one good solution to deal with emails: batch-process them too.

Set aside time limited time-slots for nothing but email and other messages and refrain from looking at them outside these slots. In "BrainChains" I explains a lot of tips, tricks and examples that can make you more efficient in dealing with emails, but batch-processing is where it all starts.

Using a phone while driving is for badly informed people or blockheads

Finally, the most dangerous way of always being connected and multitasking: doing so when you're driving your car. The research is overwhelming and scary, and the conclusion is loud and clear. Using a phone while driving increases the risk of an accident 8 to 23 times. **Hands-free or voice commanded does not make a difference at all, because it is your brain that is the bottleneck**. I know this does not sound nice, but to keep using a phone while driving once you know this is pure stupidity. In "BrainChains" I answer all the questions and objections people have, like "but what is the difference with talking with a passenger".

This kind of multitasking is so utterly dangerous that responsible companies, and especially the safety conscious production companies, should make a ban on the use of ICT while driving part of their company-wide safety policy. They should not only do it for the safety of their employees, but also to avoid an increasing risk of expensive litigation. It is a very good thing that more and more of the best companies in the world are doing this.

The technology is great; the problem is the way we use it

The solution is certainly not to throw our spectacular IT technologies overboard and return to the time of quills and dip pens. Modern technology is fantastic; the big problem is the way we use it.

The challenge to achieve optimal intellectual productivity is to limit the time spent doing fragmented, hyper-connected, stressful multitasking and to create time to disconnect, right-task, relax and let your brain function at its best.

THE THREE COMMANDMENTS

Rule nr 1

Ruthlessly, radically, eradicate switches

Rule nr 2

Disconnect to reflect

Rule nr 3

Disconnect for a break

To save a life, maybe your own

NEVER EVER use ICT while driving!

It is the responsibility of the executives to provide a working environment that makes this possible.

The Problem:
BRAIN-HOSTILE OFFICES

Before we get into this subject, let me be clear about two things. First of all, I am neither an architect nor an executive and I do not develop nor sell office equipment. I never worked in an open office and usually had my own office or shared one with only one other person.

When I talk about offices, I am looking at them from the point of view of what I learned from research carried out in different fields, about the abilities and limits of the human brain and about the innate needs of knowledge workers. I also learned about this issue during my workshops, from feedback on my keynote speeches, from coaching managers and other professionals and from a survey among 1100 professionals, half of them managers

In principle, the case for very good offices is clear and simple. The quality of the office has a major impact on the performance of brainworkers. You do not need thousands of studies about the impact of the office on people's performance to be convinced of this.

And yet almost every single time I deal with the subject of the other four BrainChains in workshops or lectures, there are participants who complain that the major factor undermining their brainwork is the open offices they have to endure.

As I explored the subject, it became increasingly clear that these people are right. The best way to undermine intellectual productivity is to stack brainworkers in open offices. Open offices are totally unfit for brainwork because they make focus, attention, concentration and reflection very stressful, if not impossible, and most often unnecessarily exhausting. Nonetheless, 70% of office workers in the USA work in open offices and new ones are still being built[5].

"Open offices: the solution is worse than the problem."

The conclusions or researchers in their own words

In 1993 I wrote:

> *"Many modern buildings, especially office blocks, make their inhabitants psychologically and physically ill because they fail to take account of the primitive (wo)man in all of us and his/her very fundamental, deeply ingrained needs."*

T.Compernolle: Stress: Friend and Foe 1993

What did I learn from the research about this issue in the last 25 years?

Let me just quote a few conclusions of scientific research and research reviews.

They speak for themselves.

There are many more, but the continuous and consistent repetition of the same conclusions would make this list very boring.

Employees who work in open-plan offices reported lower levels of job satisfaction, subjective well-being, and ease of interaction with co-workers than employees who work in cellular or shared-room offices. Therefore, decision-makers should consider the impact of open office environment on employees rather than focusing solely on cost-effective office layout, flexibility, and productivity

Otterbring T, and co 2018[6]

Our systematic review found that, compared with individual offices, *the introduction of shared or open-plan office space is remarkably consistent in its consequences,* **with every study reporting deleterious effects on employees' health.**

Ann Richardson and co 2017[7]

[In our literature review we found that] **avoiding distraction is more important than opportunities for interaction** for workers performing complex tasks, with reported distraction frequency highest among open-plan office occupants and lowest in single-room occupants.

Al Horr and co 2016[8]

"[Our systematic review of the literature shows that] open-plan offices may **adversely affect an organization's cost-efficiency** as well as the work conditions and well-being of office workers.

De Croon E, and co 2005[9]

"The findings from an extensive body of research, suggest that open plan offices do not generally support advocates' blanket claims of improved communication, satisfaction and productivity. In fact, most findings suggest the exact opposite."

George Mylonas and Jane Carstairs 2010

"...the open-plan office is not recommended for professional workers."

Anu Kaarlela-Tuomaala, 2009[10]

"In short, rather than prompting increasingly vibrant face-to-face collaboration, open architecture appeared to **trigger a natural human response to socially withdraw** *from officemates* and interact instead over email and Instant Messaging."

Ethan S. Bernstein, Stephen Turban 2018[11]

"*Our results categorically contradict the industry-accepted wisdom that open-plan layout enhances communication between colleagues and improves occupants' overall work environmental satisfaction.* This study showed that occupants' satisfaction on the interaction issue was actually higher for occupants of private offices ..."

Jonathan Kim and Richard DeDear 2013[12]

"Conclusion. Occupants sharing an office and occupants in open-plan offices (>6 occupants) had **significantly more days of sickness absence than occupants in cellular offices.**"

Pejtersen JH,and co 2011[13].

"The data show that in all categories and for most questions, employees appear to be negatively affected by the relocation to open offices, reporting decreases in their satisfaction with the physical environment, increases in physical stress, decreased team member relations and lower perceived job performance. *These results clearly indicate that not only was there an initial decrease ... the employees did not adapt to the new office environment but rather continued to find the increase in the number of disturbances and distractions counterproductive.*"

Aoife Brennan and co 2002[14]

"We found that, as work environments became more shared (**with hot-desking being at the extreme end of the continuum),** not only were there increases in demands, but co-worker friendships were not improved and perceptions of supervisory support decreased".

Rachel L. Morrison and Keith A. Macky 2018

"Such designs are argued to provide a flexible working environment, to offer space and cost savings and to promote communication between office occupants.

However, research suggests that open-plan office occupants may experience a lack of both visual and acoustical privacy and an ***increase in the amount of unwanted distractions and interruptions. In addition, the proposed benefits regarding improved communication are often not realized.***

Furthermore, open-plan occupants sometimes experience unfavorable ambient conditions, partly because of the lack of control resulting from a shared office space."

Kate Charles and Jennifer Veitch 2002[15].

"Research evidence shows that employees face a multitude of problems such as the loss of privacy, loss of identity, low work productivity, various health issues, overstimulation and low job satisfaction when working in an open-plan work environment."

Vinesh G. Oommen, Mike Knowles, Isabella Zhao 2008[16]

"There is a need for awareness of the unpredictability of spatial design, and ***simplistic views of openness as unequivocally leading to flexibility, innovation and other favorable or desirable organizational outcomes need to be challenged.*** Furthermore, *the findings also show how strategic attempts to plan for flexibility can **backfire** and that flexibility along one dimension within the organization can imply a reduction along another dimension."*

Sara Värlander 2012[17]

"Overall satisfaction with the workspace significantly improved self-estimated job performance... *The improvement of building features such as* **amount of space, visual privacy and noise level offered the highest chance to improve satisfaction with workspace.**" In 10-year survey of 50,000 office workers

Pawel Wargocki and co 2012[18]

"... **irrelevant speech contributes to mental workload, poor performance, stress, and fatigue.** Certain dispositional variables related to sustained attention might exacerbate the effects of speech-related noise."

Smith-Jackson, T.L. and Klein, K.W., 2009[19].

> *"A man doesn't know what he knows, until he knows what he doesn't know."*
>
> *Mark Twain*

Is it so hard for executives who every day, in their private office, experience the positive impact of privacy on their intellectual productivity, to imagine that this could also be true for the brainwork of their employees?

Is it so hard to imagine that it is difficult, if not impossible, to concentrate, analyse, synthesize, reflect, in fact do anything but routine work, when you are sitting in an office being constantly interrupted, continuously overhearing phone conversations and being disturbed by the most irritating and loud ringtones, music from your neighbours' headphones, people passing by all the time, cursing, conversations and chit-chatting around you?

As a senior manager, you have to be uncaring or totally misinformed about the needs of human beings and never have been forced to do difficult intellectual work in an open office, to imagine that an open office is the right environment to increase intellectual productivity.

> *"Employees are intellectual workers. But for all the wrong reasons companies keep building offices that ruin their intellectual productivity* and that is a very polite way to express myself."

Offices that abuse our inner savannah dweller

As I wrote in "Stress: Friend and Foe" in 1993 designing a worker-friendly office is not easy. Following the principal of the survival of the fittest, over hundreds of thousands of years, the human-being developed many qualities and traits that helped to procreate and survive in a life-threatening world, by moving about outdoors, harvesting plants, hunting, scavenging, and tilling the soil.

Now, in the developed world, basic survival is secured, and our work consists of sitting indoors in boring rooms, staring at screens, frenetically moving our fingers, and having meetings in concrete caves talking about subjects with no direct link with our survival or procreation.

In evolutionary terms, the change from roaming outdoors to sitting the whole day in concrete boxes, happened so fast that the traits we developed as savannah-dwellers did not have time to adapt.

A survey revealed that one in four office workers in Belgium regularly suffered from a combination of the following symptoms: exhaustion (30%), listlessness (16%), headaches (31%), irritated or weeping eyes (97%), dry eyes (9%), irritated or runny nose (11%), blocked nose (16%), dry throat (31%) and flu-like symptoms (16%).

You might think, `So what? I sometimes get those too.' But what is remarkable is that these symptoms disappeared as soon as the workers left the building they work in.

These are complaints caused by the building: the so-called Sick Building[20].

At first the symptoms of "Sick-building Syndrome" where attributed to pollutants in the air re-circulated by air-conditioning.

Later it became evident that it is not only physical pollutants which may cause disease.

Many modern office buildings, especially open offices, are set up to make it impossible for brainworkers to realize the optimal quantity and quality of brainwork because they fail to take account of the very fundamental, innate needs of our inner savannah dweller, the cave(wo)man inside all of us.

> *"Two ways companies ruin intellectual productivity: stalking and stacking their brainworkers. Stalking them by expecting them to always be connected, and stacking them in open offices"*

For millions of years people have lived in the open air. Over millions of generations, through a selection process where only the fittest have survived and procreated, the whole human organism has therefore adapted to survive life-threatening nature.

In evolutionary terms it is only very recently that we started spending most of our time inside our towns, houses, rooms and offices, often without any contact with the nature we became fundamentally adapted to, shut up like animals in an old-fashioned zoo. But the inner savannah dweller cannot undo or unlearn in just a few years the genetic mechanisms acquired over millions of years. Our organism has just not had time to adapt itself to this modern life. We therefore need to adapt the environment to the needs of our inner savannah dweller.

Our inner savannah dweller can become listless, lacking in concentration or constantly tense in an inappropriate working environment. The most disturbing factor that most brainworkers consciously experience as an obstacle for delivering excellent brainwork is noise. Noise should clearly be regarded and tackled as a very unhealthy pollutant if not poison for the brain.

But not only noise. Other factors also have a negative impact, even if we are not consciously aware of them. Here are just a few examples. You can read more about them in my book "Stress: Friend and Foe"[21].

Lack of a clearly defined territory.
Noise and conversations constantly invade the workspace. Others can walk in and out of the space uninvited, and people pass by all the time, too close for the internal cave(wo)man to feel safe.

Our inner savannah dweller not only needs a clearly defined territory, but also a safe place without unwanted acoustical, visual or sensory intrusions. The absence of walls, of privacy, gives the savannah dweller a feeling of always being watched, never being safe. This keeps the alarm-system on all the time and creates an unhealthy, continuous, low background stress.

Excess social density.
This territorial problem is often made worse by an excess of social density: too many people packed together. The social density we can endure is different from person to person and from culture to culture, but there are clear limits. A little too much space is not a problem, but a space that is just a little too small will make you uncomfortable. The higher the social density, the lower the satisfaction[22]. Modern offices are too rigid to allow brainworkers to

adapt the size of their privacy "bubble" to their personal and cultural needs.

Monotonous surroundings.
Monotonous noise, monotonous temperature, monotonous smell, monotonous views and blank walls. If, on top of all that, work is monotonous too, your senses will crave stimulation and you will escape to the continuous little shots of dopamine provided by emails, other messages and especially the antisocial-media.

Lack of meaningful visual stimuli.
The savannah dweller, after living in the wild for millions of years, is very attached to greenery, seeing the horizon, clouds and the sky.

The circulation of smells.
can make us become tense without realizing it has anything to do with artificial smell.

"It's the only place left
that's not open plan!"

Continuous vibrations.
If the frequency changes, as it does with the changing wind strength or wind direction, then the primitive (wo) man in you may become alarmed and tense, even though you are not conscious of the cause.

Lack of influence on your environment.
One of the most important factors that increases stress is not having any influence on your environment, such as being able to adjust the temperature, music, air, light etc...to personal needs.

Offices that undermine intellectual productivity

How to reduce footprint while creating an environment that supports brainwork
The challenge for executives is that with the great flexibility that ICT provides and more people working only part of the time at their desks, much office space is considered to be wasted and that this is too expensive. The open plan office obviously is the cheapest and easiest solution.

Executives and architects, however, are too often totally uninformed about the "operating instructions" of human beings in general and brainworkers and their brains more specifically. Then, with only short term cost cutting in mind, too many companies are not aware of the long term waste of money resulting from underperformance, when they build or rent these cheap offices that are clearly very brain-hostile.

As a result, rationalizing the use of office space often turns out to be very irrational.

The challenge is to reduce the footprint of an office while providing an environment that enhances brainwork instead of ruining it. To do this executives and architects should learn about the fundamental directions for use of brainworkers and the human brain. Only then will they be able to build the right flexible environment with spaces adapted to the many different kinds of work brainworkers do.

Most offices are built on an erroneous premise, with wrong priorities

Actually, in most offices the base camp for brainworkers is one with very low privacy; privacy in the sense of being protected against any unsolicited sensory distractions and as we will see further on, noise and especially phone-calls are the worst. (In "BrainChains" I explain in depth the extremely huge cost of these distractions.) This low privacy is "sold" to workers as a means to increase communication and collaboration. As we will see further on, even that idea is wrong. Lack of privacy increases chitchatting, while decreasing real conversations and increasing emailing[23].

I learned from my review that **only when privacy is granted communication will improve, if not the increased contact is just reflection-destroying hubbub**.

Some (young) people enjoy the brouhaha, but do not know how bad it is for their intellectual performance and productivity.

From this brainwork-hostile base-camp, brainworkers can then sometimes escape to quiet spaces to do work that needs concentration. In many companies however, even this escape is not provided.

After studying the research literature my conclusion is very clear: this is exactly the opposite of what brainworkers need to be optimally productive. As we will discuss in more detail later, **the priority of an office for brainworkers doing non-routine work should focus and privacy, not contact.** This does not necessarily mean they need a personal office, as long as sufficient well in-

47

sulated spaces (the Latin word insula means island) are provided for people who need to concentrate or who want to have a real conversation without disturbing others. I also learned that the most important and most expensive aspect of this brainwork enhancing privacy is protection against noise and above all against phone conversations.

> *"Do the telephone test: If you are doing work that needs concentration and you can hear other people making phone calls, you are in the wrong office."*

Since most brainwork needs focus, there should be enough of these brainwork spaces so that people can make these their basecamp. **With focus in the front of their mind, executives and architects can then design the rest of the office in such a way that as soon as people leave their brainwork-enhancing basecamp, contact becomes unavoidable.**

As you will see further on, designing such a brainwork enhancing office is not a zero sum game and not even a dilemma. Except for executives who see an office as nothing but an immediate cost, instead of an investment in their brainworkers to get a big return of more and better brainwork.

In any case it makes no financial sense whatsoever to invest most of your money in hiring the best and the brightest and then warehousing them in a working environment that severely reduces their productivity. To say it politely: this is what the English call "penny wise and extremely pound foolish".

Most brainworkers hate their open office because they know it decreases their intellectual productivity, health and...collaboration.

The open office has become the predominant office layout. The purpose of the open-plan office is to be flexible with regards to organizational change and to handle change without any need for reconstruction[24]. It also drastically decreases the footprint and maintenance costs per employee. They are also sold as a solution to improve collaboration and communication, but the main driver is most often cost cutting.

Up to 90% of office workers hate their open offices because there is too much distraction and too much noise. The larger the office, the less people like them[25]. People often speak about 'Cubicle Hell', 'Brain Warehouses', 'Brain Jails' and even 'Brain Torture Chambers'. Although his drawings are very primitive and visually repetitive, the depiction of Dilbert in this cubicle hell clearly touched a raw nerve and made Scott Adams one of the most successful modern cartoonists[26].

What kind of an office would be the best for you to do your daily work?

my own personal office at work (not shared with anybody)	560	52%
an office shared with 1 to 3 people	229	21%
an office shared with 4 to 10 people without individual cubicles	35	3%
an office shared with 4 to 10 people with individual cubicles	44	4%
an individual cubicle in an open office with 20 people or less	26	2%
an individual cubicle in an open office with 21 people or more	10	1%
an open office with 20 people or less ; without individual cubicle	18	2%
an open office with 21 people or more ; without individual cubicle	8	1%
a home office for myself	120	11%
Other	27	3%

(n=1078, ± 50/50 managers/other professionals)

In my own survey amongst 1100 professionals, half of them managers, only 13% consider an open office a good place to work!

If they have to do difficult intellectual work, 65% do it at home, not by preference but by necessity because it is impossible to do this type of work in the office. This is the opinion of the best and the brightest their companies were able to hire. Why don't companies listen to them, even not when research supports their opinion?

Other interesting statistics include that only 38% of employees are proud enough of their office to show it to an important customer and half of office workers would work an extra hour if they had a better work environment[27].

An increasing number of people are starting to work from home. Why? Because of the rarely mentioned advantage of flexwork: it allows people to escape their horrible offices. They can escape their exhausting brain-jail, that some even call their brain-torture chamber, even if they would really prefer to work in a good office alongside their colleagues.

LOW PRIVACY = LOW PRODUCTIVITY !

Lack of Architectural PRIVACY

Interruptions
Lack of Perceived Privacy:
Noise is #1
Noise #1= Phone

Cognitive/emotional Exhaustion

ADAPT PRIVACY TO THE TASK !
= To the level of attention and concentration needed

I recently spoke to a young very successful manager who said that since her department had moved to an open-office plan, she comes home in the evening totally exhausted, even though nothing has changed in her workload. Her house is not an ideal place to work at all, but she has nonetheless started to work from home, not by choice, but to escape the office.

In another case, in a workshop with managers of a global company, I jokingly used the word brain-prison to describe their feedback about their office. One of the participants reacted with great frustration: "You are being too nice. The open offices we got two years ago are not brain-prisons that prevent our brains from performing at their best and from communicating. They are brain-torture-chambers because not only do I perform well below my intellectual potential and complete less work in a day, but I leave the office exhausted and often with a headache, even though my workload hasn't changed. I never had this problem before when we had offices for maximal three people". His colleagues agreed. These were not people abused in a call centre; they were very highly skilled professionals, engineers, economists, accountants and a few HR specialists, about half of them managers earning millions for their company.

Why do companies impose this to their most important asset, to their most important competitive advantage, their knowledge workers? My story becomes repetitive: **Companies hire the best brains they can find and then do not listen to them when they tell their offices undermine their productivity.**

The idea of the open office is forced onto employees with arguments that they encourage more flexibility, creativity, social interaction, informal communication, increased job satisfaction and collaboration. In Dutch and German, open offices are even called "office garden" and "office countryside" (Kantoortuin and Bürolandschaft, respectively). In the light of the available research about the negative impact on satisfaction and intellectual productivity this is a new height in cynical business lingo.

In most open offices, even communication is worse.

The argument that the open office "improves communication and collaboration" turns out to be true only to a very small extent: it takes significantly less time to get an answer to a question from a peer or a manager and there is indeed an increase in contacts, but... these are short and superficial[28]. Open offices have a negative impact on collaboration and communication when the privacy and focus of the brainworkers fails to be taken into account. People will only truly collaborate and share information when their focus is protected by sufficient privacy![29] Moreover, because of the lack of privacy or because people do not want to disturb each other, open offices often hinder important communication and information sharing more than private offices do.

The Open Office Fallacy
The more open, the more communication

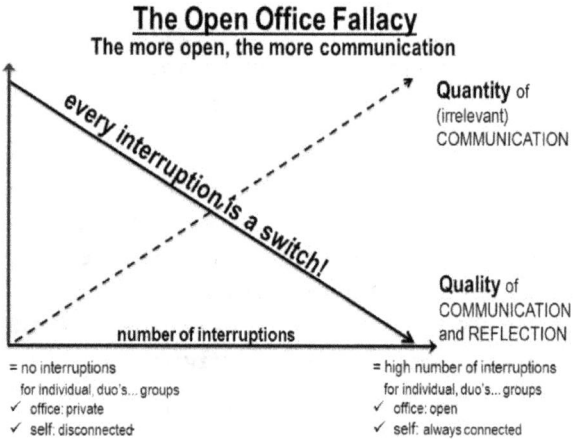

every interruption is a switch!

Quantity of (irrelevant) COMMUNICATION

Quality of COMMUNICATION and REFLECTION

number of interruptions

= no interruptions
 for individual, duo's... groups
 ✓ office: private
 ✓ self: disconnected

= high number of interruptions
 for individual, duo's... groups
 ✓ office: open
 ✓ self: always connected

In reality:
The more open, the more AND the worse communication

If you have a communication problem in your company, open offices will not resolve it, on the contrary, the risk is high that they will make it worse.

In 2018 a sophisticated research by Bernstein and Turban from Harvard, using digital data from advanced wearable devices and from electronic communication servers, showed that: *"rather than prompting increasingly vibrant face-to-face collaboration, open architecture appeared to trigger a natural human response to socially withdraw from officemates and interact instead over email and IM"*

Optimal collaboration and communication first need privacy and focus. As I will explain in the chapter about solutions, this is neither a contradiction, nor a dilemma or a zero-sum game, but a question of the right priorities. The most significant negative factor is a lack of privacy, which leads to continuous distractions and therefore a lack of focus. The result is a very significant drop in efficiency, which means that workers take more time and do lower-quality work. Privacy in this context means being protected from unwanted intrusions and interruptions through any of our senses. Of these, noise and especially hearing the phone calls of others, has the worst impact of all because we are defenceless against it.

In most open offices, the pain is much greater than the gain. Intellectual productivity diminishes due to unwanted social contact, continuous distractions, cognitive overload, noise, unnecessary stress and their negative impact on cognitive processes, cognitive task performance and job satisfaction.

Open offices maximize interruptions and disturbances, make difficult intellectual work impossible and make continuous task-switching unavoidable[30].

They lead to high turnover or the intention to leave the company at the first opportunity. They cause an increase in absenteeism and health problems such as infections and high blood pressure. People in open offices have 62% more sick days[31].

If as a manager the wellbeing of your people is not your top priority, you might be interested in the high cost and the even higher opportunity costs.

> *If you cut up a large diamond into little bits, it will entirely lose the value it had as a whole; and an army divided up into small bodies of soldiers loses all its strength. So a great intellect sinks to the level of an ordinary one as soon as it is interrupted and disturbed, its attention distracted and drawn off from the matter in hand; for its superiority depends upon its power of concentration — of bringing all its strength to bear upon one theme, in the same way as a concave mirror collects into one point all the rays of light that strike upon it... That is why distinguished minds have always shown such an extreme dislike to disturbance in any form, as something that breaks in upon and distracts their thoughts.*

Arthur Schopenhauer: On Noise. 1851[32]

The conclusion is simple: most open offices significantly undermine the quantity and quality of the performance of brainworkers mainly because they eliminate focus[33],[34]. To make things even worse, it was recently discovered that in open offices people also self-interrupt more often[35]! A real double-whammy against intellectual productivity!

Conclusion: For intellectual work, open offices are the wrong solution.

It is very clear that when designing offices the motto must be: focus first, collaboration second. This will not only optimize the knowledge work being done but also improve collaboration!

There is only one exception to this rule: routine work. Some distraction helps to prevent this work from becoming too boring and increases the performance and feeling of wellbeing.

Look at it from the bright side:

Employees who can focus are 57% more effective in collaboration, 88% more so in learning, 42% in socializing, 31% in innovation and they have a 31% higher job satisfaction[36]

Why open offices have a very bad influence on brainwork

The core of the problem is that our thinking brain cannot multitask. When we switch between tasks or try to do two things at the same time, our thinking-brain must switch each time. In my books "BrainChains" and "How to Unchain Your Brain" I explain the exact mechanism in more detail.

SERIAL MULTITASKING: switching cost = huge loss of time

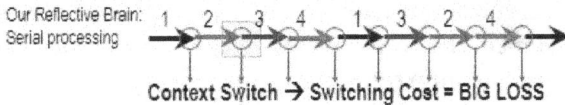

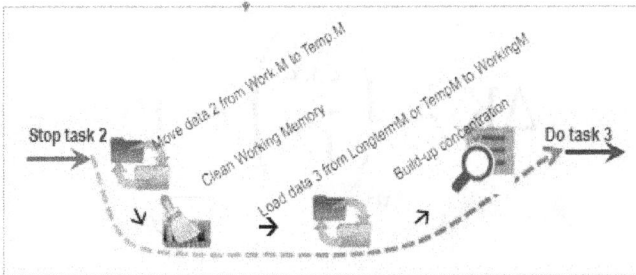

Our Reflective Brain: Serial processing 1 2 3 4 1 3 2 4

Context Switch → Switching Cost = BIG LOSS

Stop task 2 — Move data 2 from Work M to Temp M — Clean Working Memory — Load data 3 from LongtermM or TempM to WorkingM — Build-up concentration — Do task 3

TASK-SWITCHING = longer + more time, energy, mistakes and stress

longer — loss — longer — loss — longer — loss 235

Every interruption forces the thinking brain to switch. At every switch the brain has to transfer the information it was dealing with from working memory to temporary memory. It then has to clean working memory to prevent the two tasks from interfering with each other. Then it has to transfer the information needed for the next task (or for dealing with an interruption) from long-term memory to working memory and take some time to build up concentration again. It's easy to imagine that **every switch costs energy, memory, efficiency, productivity and stress.** But the cost is much higher than you think.

Moreover, the less the subjects of the tasks are related the bigger the loss. Therefore the switches are called context-switches. It depends on the relationship of the two subjects how big the loss is.

Research by W.Pillen at the University of Delft with several thousands of office workers shows that in open offices they are interrupted every two minutes on average. Yes, this is no typo: every two (2) minutes!

Every interruption forces our thinking-brain to make a switch. Hence, the core flaw and vice of open offices are the continuous interruptions.

$$\Delta K \approx \left(\frac{At}{I^2} \right) + Pt$$

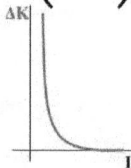

K= Knowledge acquisition (intellectual productivity, innovation, learning ...)
A= Attention P= Pause offscreen t= time
I = Interruptions

To summarize the challenge in a formula: the intellectual productivity of an office worker is proportional to the duration of her attention divided by the square of the interruptions plus the time she takes to have regular disconnected, screenfree pauses.

Did you know that when a code writer is interrupted for a telephone call, it costs him on average twenty minutes to get back on the original level of concentration?

Noise is one of the worst possible influences on intellectual productivity and it undermines health too

In a discussion with a manager he pulled a list from the Internet to convince me that office noise isn't that bad after all because there's only 10% more noise than in a living room. The list looked like this:

Decibel	Environment
40	Library
50	Living room in suburban area
60	Typical business office
70	Telephone ringing at 2m
70	Conversational speech
80	Average traffic on a street corner

This has happened a few more times since. Therefore, before we go on to discuss noise, I'd like to rectify this very common mistake in interpreting this list and the numbers.

The Decibel scale is a logarithmic one. An increase of 10 decibels does not mean **10%** more but **10 times more**. Hence, a difference of 10dB between two types of offices or improving the decibel level in an office by 10dB is very significant. It's also worth noting that office noise above 50dB is very irritating for 40% of people.

I'd also like to emphasize that hearing noises and listening to sounds are two totally different phenomena that even happen in two different brain systems.

Listening engages our thinking-brain; it requires top-down attention. Hearing noise engages our reflex-brain no matter whether we want it or not, it engages the bottom-up attention of our stimulus driven reflex-brain. Therefore, listening and hearing can even be in conflict, for example when you try to listen to a colleague while you can hear somebody on the phone in the next cubicle.

> *"Noise is the most impertinent of all forms of interruption. It is not only an interruption, but also a disruption of thought. Of course, where there is nothing to interrupt, noise will not be so particularly painful.*

Arthur Schopenhauer: On Noise. 1851[37]

Most intellectual work done by office workers needs a quiet environment with as little distraction as possible. The more difficult the task, the more important this is.

When brainworkers hate their open offices, they most often complain about the noise (noise defined as unwanted sound), and they are right. Noise has the most and proven negative influence, not only on job satisfaction but also on intellectual performance and productivity[38]. This is also the case even if the noise doesn't consciously seem to bother people or if people think they have adapted to it. In a task to memorize words or to do simple arithmetic, for example, more noise resulted in fewer words remembered, more mistakes made and being more tired[39]. This must be a rather fundamental, genetic phenomenon, and not just a question of subjective appraisal, because even rats perform worse on learning tasks in a noisy environment[40].

Only when the work is boring does some noise help to stay concentrated, especially for extraverts[41.] If there is not much work stress, then the level of noise does not make much of a difference in terms of job satisfaction, organizational commitment or self-reported health.

It becomes very significant when work stress is high[42]. Hence, noisy open offices are only acceptable for boring or non-stressful work.

> **"Noisy open offices are a disaster, except for boring or stressfree work"**

Noise also causes health problems and unhealthy stress. In the past, most research was about problems caused by rather loud noise, like traffic, cars, machines and planes. Now, the interest in the health consequences has moved from high decibel noise to lower but chronic noise, such as that experienced in offices. Low noise too turns out to be bad for our health[43]. In noise-sensitive people, for example, just the exposure during two hours to low-frequency continuous ventilation noise already increases stress hormones[44]. A lot of attention has been given to the study of the consequences for our cardiovascular system, probably because it is rather easy to measure blood pressure and the composition of the blood.

For example, 40 female clerical workers were randomly assigned for three hours either to a quiet office set-up or to a set-up with the typical low-intensity noise of open offices. Subjectively, the ones with the noise did not experience more stress... and yet the stress hormones in their blood were nonetheless significantly more elevated (!). They also gave up solving a puzzle more quickly after the experience, clearly showing a decrease in willpower and brain energy (See "BrainChains": BrainChain 1).

By the way, other negative health consequences were due to the fact that they also made fewer ergonomic, postural adjustments in their computer workstation[45]. The extra concentration needed to compensate for the noise also caused more strain on their body (See "BrainChains": BrainChain-3).

Problems associated with noise are not only of significance for those working in an office or on the shopfloor. They are also an issue, for example, for teachers in a classroom. Teachers working in classrooms with bad acoustics, when compared with those in classrooms with good acoustics, report lower job satisfaction, a lack of energy after work, a desire to leave their job, a lack of motivation and sleepiness.[46]

> *"There are people, it is true — nay, a great many people — who smile at such things, because they are not sensitive to noise; but they are just the very people who are also not sensitive to argument, or thought, or poetry, or art, in a word, to any kind of intellectual influence. The reason of it is that the tissue of their brains is of a very rough and coarse quality. On the other hand, noise is a torture to intellectual people.*

Arthur Schopenhauer: On Noise. 1851[47]

Noise is a typical disturbance that employees cannot influence, and having no influence on a source of stress, feeling powerless, greatly increases the negative impact of any source of stress[48]. Human beings cannot close their ears, cannot shut off hearing, not even when they sleep! Hearing is a very automatic, fast attention-grabber; it bypasses our thinking-brain.

Not being able to close their ears was important for the survival of savannah dwellers. Hearing was the ultimate alarm system, never to be shut down. We still react to noise like our ancestors. When there is a noise after a period of silence, it will always catch our attention, regardless of whether we want it to or not, regardless of whether we are conscious of it or not. This is called the "orientation reflex". When it is a sudden loud noise it is called the "startling reflex", which can even be observed when people are not conscious of the noise, for example when they are sleeping.

So, even if you think you have adapted to the noise in your office, sudden noises will always activate your nervous and endocrine system.

The noise in an office and especially the conversations going on around us are irregular, they alternate with silence and as a result we never really habituate[49].

Trying to analyse a contract or study a spreadsheet with market data in an open office is like reading a non-fiction book in a loud bar. Hence, many people even prefer the relative calm of a coffee shop, rather than the office, to get some work done.

From conversations with people working in open offices and from some Googling and YouTubing about office noise aggression, I have learned that noise frequently makes people feel or even act aggressively or at least impolitely.

The angry reactions are very similar to when people have to listen night and day to the music of neighbours who insist on playing their favourite tracks at top volume.

This anger towards noise also probably stems from our history in the savannah when it might often have signalled an intrusion into our territory. Just the exposure to low level low frequency noise (frequency of ventilating system) resulted in a lower social orientation (more disagreeable, less co-operative, helpful) and a tendency to lower pleasantness as compared to the mid frequency noise exposure[50].

Occasionally it happens that some slight but constant noise continues to bother and distract me for a time before I become distinctly conscious of it. All I feel is a steady increase in the labor of thinking — just as though I were trying to walk with a weight on my foot.

Arthur Schopenhauer: On Noise. 1851[51]

Amongst the noises, intelligible speech is the most distracting.

When you can understand what other people are saying, your intellectual productivity immediately drops by 50 to 60%[52], except when you are really in "flow", a state of total absorption in your task, a state that is very unlikely to happen in an open office because of the high level of concentration and enjoyment in your task that is required. The more intelligible the speech, be it from overhearing one half of a conversation, monologues or dialogues, the more it ruins intellectual productivity[53].

The effect of hearing speech is based on two mechanisms that both reduce performance: it disturbs cognitive processing and it causes an automatic orientation reflex that interrupts your attention.

As office noise is not continuous but rather contains unpredictable periods of silence and speech with varying intelligibility, one cannot permanently become accustomed to office noise.

The worst is overhearing a phone conversation.

Let's call these "demilogues". This word does not exist, but it is useful in this context to differentiate them from monologues and dialogues.

Monologues and dialogues are distracting
Demilogues most significantly harm attention

M-500

Demilogues are the worst disturbances, even much more distracting and difficult to block out than monologues and dialogues[54].

There are several reasons for this. One is that each time the other person starts talking it's new and somewhat unexpected and it ends with a micro-cliff-hanger that keeps us engaged during the brief silence (More on this in the chapter on addiction to being connected in "Brain-Chains"). The other reason is that when we hear a demilogue the orientation reflex response is stronger than in a monologue or dialogue. This is because a demilogue is an alternation of speech and silence, resulting in an almost unavoidable orientation reflex each time the speech starts after a period of silence. A crucial problem is that this reflex cannot be eliminated.

The Lombard effect makes people speaking louder than necessary

I was once interviewed for TV in a noisy cafeteria. The TV crew told me that I did not have to speak so loudly. I realized perfectly well that with the microphone in front of my face, I did not need to speak so loudly, but again and again I did it anyway without realizing.

This phenomenon, which often worsens the office situation, is the so-called **Lombard effect**. It refers to the fact that **the noisier the environment, the louder we speak**, even if it is not necessary for the conversation we are having with a person sitting next to us. This also happens, for example, when somebody speaking on the phone in a noisy room speaks very loudly, even when the person on the other end asks him to speak more softly because the conversation is perfectly clear at the other end and the loud voice is experienced as shouting.

Masking noise makes it worse.

Depending on the acoustic qualities of the room the sound produced will be attenuated on its way from the source to the listener, who will only hear it when it is louder than the background noise.

From there comes the idea of increasing the background noise in such a way that it is no longer consciously perceived but still masks the other sounds so that these are no longer a distraction.

Masking-noise seems to help sometimes in masking speech[55], but as I will describe in the chapter about solutions, it is very difficult to get right. It is certainly no panacea to resolve the acoustic problems of a badly designed office.

Lack of Architectural Privacy   Lack of Perceived Privacy: NOISE!   Cognitive/Emotional Exhaustion

More and more people bring earplugs, noise-cancelling headphones and personal masking-noise generators to the office because they suffer from the office noise (More on this in Section 3).

What amazes me is that company managers do not see this as a signal that something is wrong with the working environment; after all, people are willing to pay $300 and go against social conventions of putting on headphones to make their work environment a little more bearable. I think this is a clear indictment not just of the lack of silence in offices, but also of the ignorance or the lack of listening or the penny-wise pound-foolishness of the executives who build or lease these offices.

The importance of having some influence on the work environment

There is ample research about the importance of high-quality temperature, ventilation and lighting systems in offices, and yet surprisingly often they are designed badly. What is always forgotten is the extremely high psychological importance of being able to influence these factors yourself. Having some control over them makes even non-ideal temperatures and lighting easier to bear.

Being able to influence the sources of our stress is a highly important factor in managing our stress in general.

In my workshops and presentations I often give an excellent example of some of the very rare architects who are aware of these fundamental needs of human beings: Henry Cobb and Yvonne Szeto (of Pei Cobb Freed & Partners), who designed the beautiful headquarters of a bank.

On my first visit there I discovered they had designed little windows of about 30cm by 20cm that people could open and yet small enough not to disturb the central air-conditioning. When I tell engineers or managers about this, they never guess that the architects designed this to give people a feeling of having some control over their working environment.

The bank's facilities management didn't realize this either and a few years later, failing to understand the important psychological reason for these "useless" little windows, they blocked them so that they can no longer be opened. For engineers, who are trained in physics, this is a perfectly rational action. It is very irrational, however, if you know something about the directions for use of human beings. (More on the importance of a feeling of control the work environment in the section about solutions of this booklet and in BrainChain 3 of "BrainChains").

Office workers are almost never involved in the planning phase of a new building and so have very little, if any, influence on the fundamental layout of their future offices. A root problem is that these offices are developed and built for the company, not for the workers. **The workers have to adapt to the office instead of the other way around, even if the office makes it impossible to be really productive.**

Executives will react with "we cannot adapt our plans to 1,000 wishes". Well, first of all, as we will see in the solutions chapter, you can. Second, different people have different wishes, but they all have some basic innate needs in common. Third, there is a vast amount of research showing that you can build an office that comes much closer to being optimal for the brainwork of the majority.

As I explained in the foreword, a new office is not a mere real-estate project. It is a strategic change project. As for all change projects, one of the best things that can be done to increase the engagement and the feeling of having an influence that matters, is to have a proactive policy to collect and solicit feedback and complaints about the building and to use this information to continuously improve the performance of the building and the people.

It is a continuous, never ending, trial and error learning process. With two exceptions I haven't seen any companies where this is systematically done, even in companies where continuous improvement plays an important role. I've read about the way Google tries to do this and how it considers creating the right working environment as a never ending work in progress[56]. With only a few exceptions, this aspect of continuous improvement has not had much attention from architects and researchers either[57].

Help the Multitaskers and the Generation Y and following generations

Special attention should be given to young workers born in the early eighties, and those who come after them.

In general they experience the noise, the lack of privacy and the lack of control of their environment as negatively as their older colleagues do. Some are willing to accept this disadvantage for the advantage of the time spent socializing[58].

Others enjoy the fun and the camaraderie of an open office. Against all available scientific evidence (summarized in "BrainChains"), they are convinced that being always connected and being distracted is OK to do their work, that they are good at multitasking and that it has no negative impact on their performance.

Even if it does not bother them, it still greatly undermines their performance, especially when work requires undivided attention. In other words, they may complain less about the buzzing, distracting environment of an open office, they may even like it, but the negative impact on their intellectual productivity, when reflection is needed, is the same as for anybody else.

Generation Y may complain less about the buzzing, distracting environment of an open office, they may even like it, but the negative impact on their intellectual productivity, when reflection is needed, is the same as for anybody else.

As I described in "BrainChains", the heavy multitaskers, habitual multitaskers or hypertaskers, young and old, think about themselves that they are good at multitasking, while research very clearly shows that they are significantly worse at switching between tasks than people who multitask less. Multitaskers perform even worse in open offices, because they are worse at ignoring irrelevant distractions and getting back on track after an interruption.

Since employees can be very satisfied and very unproductive at the same time, simple satisfaction surveys are not a good basis to judge the quality of an office. It is important to measure other factors such as productivity, creativity, stress and wellbeing.

As an employee, don't blame your managers but join them to influence the top executives

There are many bad offices still being built for no other reason than driving down costs, while the messages about improving communication, collaboration and flexibility are pure baloney. Since these companies try to hire the best and the brightest, these workers are certainly intelligent enough to understand this foul play. The impact on their engagement, work satisfaction and motivation will not be positive, to say the least.

If you are an employee suffering in such a work environment, you should not blame your own manager. The managers who have to suffer the long-term pain and loss of intellectual productivity together with their workforce are different ones form the executives responsible, and rewarded, for the short-time gain of a cheap building. Instead, you should join forces with your own manager to adapt the existing office to the privacy needs of knowledge workers and to influence the planning of new offices. Your interests overlap with theirs.

"Don't expect people to think out of the box, while they are in an open office or boxed in cube.

The challenge for executives: resolving the privacy-contact and cost-investment dilemma

The cheaper the offices the more expensive they are

Let's just admit that most bad offices are built with cost cutting in mind, often nicely wrapped in company speak about the open office as an instrument for improving collaboration and blahdy blahdy blah. If you doubt this statement, talk to the victims who work in these offices, the architects who have to design them, the facilities managers who have to implement them and even the top executives who attended the planning discussions.

The sad fact is that although so many dysfunctional, if not illness-inducing, offices are built with cost cutting in mind, even the cost-cutting argument is totally irrational.

> *"The sad fact is that although so many dysfunctional, if not illness-inducing, offices are built with cost cutting in mind, even the cost-cutting argument is totally irrational."*

*I was invited to one of the world's top high-tech companies to discuss the theme of "Stress: Friend and Foe". The audience of 100 professionals, mostly engineers, asked a lot of questions about the stress caused by their offices. At one point I asked them to estimate the positive or negative influence of their new (= 4 years old) offices on their intellectual productivity: their guess was **a 40% (median) drop in productivity.***

For most of them the most frustrating counter-productive result was that they made more mistakes in the open office than when they worked undisturbed, which then took much more time to correct, not to speak of their clients' dissatisfaction.

As I'd already learned from my surveys, these very high-level professionals have to escape from their offices to be really productive! Many do their best reflecting at home, in the car, in the train or even in the coffee shop at the other side of the street, not by choice, but because their office is totally unfit for high-level brainwork.

What is even more surprising is that from the day they moved to open offices, the spontaneous job-related communication decreased (!) significantly compared with when they had individual offices or cubicles.

The main reasons were that they did not want to bother their colleagues in the room, they missed the privacy to discuss matters freely and they did not have any spare energy to invest in good discussions because the office exhausted them (and undermined their motivation).

You do not need to be an engineer to understand that the daily loss for the company, when these most highly paid engineers work at only 60% of their potential, is much higher than whatever costs were saved when these open offices were built only a few years ago.

Sadly enough, this company is not an exception, but rather the rule. **Low-cost open offices are the cheapest to build, but carry a huge productivity and opportunity cost in the medium and longer term.** It is more expensive to design flexible offices with plenty of privacy, particularly as special attention is needed to encourage contact while avoiding noise, but in the long-term the result is a huge return in productivity.

It is worse than penny wise and pound-foolish. It's even penny foolish. Let me explain

> *"Warehousing brainworkers in open offices is worse than penny wise and pound foolish. It's even penny foolish.*

The General Services Administration (GSA), responsible for government buildings in the US, made this very simple calculation: of the total cost of running an office building over 30 years, the initial construction represents 2%, the operating expenses 6% and the remaining 92% goes to paying the people inside, who earn the money for the company[59].

What is the best value for money, cutting as much as you can off the 8% total costs or getting an optimal or just a little better productivity out of the 92% cost?

What is the long-term opportunity cost of a 30-40% decrease in intellectual productivity? You don't need to be a financial genius to guess what it means for the bottom line.

Since every day executives still decide to build or lease these counter-productive offices, let me super-simplify the reasoning to give an impression of the order of magnitude of the real losses we are talking about. For simplicity I've left out all the details like the 62% more sick days taken in open offices, their negative impact on satisfaction and motivation levels and the higher staff turnover, although I learned from HR-specialists that replacing one skilled professional costs on average 100% of that individual's annual salary.

> *"Cut the cost of an office: Your company loses $5.- or more for every $1 cut.*
> *Invest more in the office: Your company gains $5.- or more for every $1 invested."*

Let me use the estimation of the GSA and exaggerate the savings while downplaying the losses. In the example below 1$ dollar can represent one million or several millions of dollars.

Let's say the total expense of running your office is $300. Your building costs are 2% or $6.- Imagine you manage to save a whopping 20% on the building costs. You do this by putting a lot more people together in one space and by limiting the investment in privacy and especially in noise reduction that is one of the major costs. You save $1.2 which is 0.4% of your total expense of $300.

Conclusion number 1:
Cutting the cost of peanuts can be nothing but peanuts.

But cutting the costs of an office is not neutral because it results in lower intellectual productivity.

Although, as you have seen in the conclusions from the research and in the example of my client above, the decline of intellectual productivity can be much higher, let's imagine that this cost cutting results in a decrease of intellectual productivity of only 10%. Given that the workers cost 90% of the total operating cost, the result is that you lose $27.- for every $1.2 you saved. A loss of about $22.- or more, for every single dollar you saved on the building, is a very bad deal for your company.

Conclusion number 2:
You miss gold nuggets when you cut the cost of peanuts

You just can't win with a bad office! Even if you manage to cut the costs of an office building to 40% of the average and this cost cutting causes only 10% less productivity, you still lose! The only solution is to avoid by all means ever building such an office.

Conclusion number 3:
A bad office is a lose-lose-lose operation

I hope you can guess who the third loser is.

Imagine that after reading this book and some further study, you build or renovate an office with not only costs in mind, but also the needs of brainworkers and their brains.

To do so, you invest 20% more than originally planned, an additional cost of $1.2. If this leads to only a 10% increase in intellectual productivity, the additional revenue is $27.-

This means that for every $1.- you invested, you gain $22.- or more.

Do you know many investments with a ROI of 22?

Conclusion number 4:
Investing in a really good office is a win-win-win operation

> *"Cutting the cost of peanuts is always peanuts*
> *Cut the cost of peanuts and you lose gold nuggets*
> *Invest peanuts in people and they will produce*
> *gold in the coffer."*

When a company plans an office, it wants to reduce the footprint of each employee, reduce the number of desks, especially in organizations where a lot of work is done outside the office, and increase communication and collaboration. There is certainly nothing wrong with that, on the contrary. The challenge is to achieve this without undermining the quality and quantity of difficult, complex intellectual work or of other brainwork like reading, analysis and writing that require prolonged periods of undisturbed, undivided attention and focus. Breaking down all the walls and squeezing in as many people as possible per square foot, however, is certainly not a solution to increase contact, communication and collaboration and certainly no way to increase productivity and profit, on the contrary.

The dilemma between privacy and contact

$$\Delta K \approx \left(\frac{At}{I^2} \right) + Pt$$

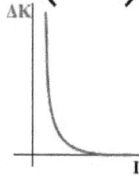

K= Knowledge acquisition (intellectual productivity, innovation, learning ...)
A= Attention P= Pause offscreen t= time
I = Interruptions

Imagine your company employs a lot of engineers. Analysing their work we discover that 50% of their work is high level intellectual solo work that needs attention and concentration: problem solving, reading, analysing, writing etc. 50% of their work is interacting, communicating with others. If you give them a personal office for the first 50%, the office will be empty 50% of the time. If you give them excellent meeting rooms, these too will be empty 50% of the time.

Obviously, for executives, the seemingly rational and cheapest solution is to put them in an open office where they can combine both tasks. This is a awful mistake.

On the one hand, the executives want to break up the isolation and reduce the cost caused by the single private offices to enhance social contact, interaction, communication and collaboration.

On the other hand, they forget that the ever-increasing level and complexity of brainwork needs ever-increasing privacy[2] to protect the focus, attention and concentration needed for analysis, synthesis, abstraction, reflection, creativity, innovation and all other kinds of non-routine brainwork.

However, focus and contact cannot be combined in one and the same space. Adding a few quiet offices to escape for tasks that require focus is not the solution.

Moreover, as we will discuss further on, without privacy the quantity of quality of the job related communication decreases.

> *"The ever-increasing level and complexity of brainwork needs ever-increasing privacy to protect the focus, attention and concentration needed for analysis, synthesis, abstraction, reflection, creativity, innovation and all other kinds of non-routine brainwork."*

For many managers, this looks like a dilemma, a zero-sum game. When the office environment maximizes privacy, focus and attention, as it does for the offices of managers and executives, it decreases the opportunities for spontaneous, impromptu contact and interaction and the layout is more expensive.

When privacy is reduced as much as possible, as is the case for the offices for the rank and file, it encourages more interaction, but creates continuous disturbances that eliminate the most valuable conditions for high-level intellectual productivity: focus and attention. The result is lower intellectual productivity, less satisfaction, higher turnover but a building that is much cheaper to build and maintain.

---

2 By "privacy" I mean the absence of all unwanted acoustic, visual and tactile contact, together with some personal influence on light, temperature and the layout of a personal space.

This zero-sum reasoning, however, is wrong. It is even wrong for the cost factor, as we have seen above. **The solution is, first of all, to see an office as an investment in people's productivity rather than as a cost and, secondly, to start with privacy as the first priority and then add contact as close a second while ensuring that it doesn't hinder privacy** (More about this in the chapter about solutions).

A history of collusion between architects and executives uninformed about the innate needs of people

Managers have to continuously think in terms of increasing revenue and cutting costs. Lacking knowledge about about the psychological needs of brainworkers and their inner savannah dweller, they see an office as a cost that is easy to cut rather than as a source of revenue. The result is that they choose the wrong offices.

- Offices where difficult and complex brainwork is impossible;

- Offices where employees can't do their most important job of thinking: thinking forward, thinking wide, thinking deep and thinking new;

- Offices they are ashamed to show to clients;

- Offices they have to escape from to be more intellectually productive and less exhausted;

- Offices that they call 'brain torture chambers';

- Offices they hate.

Maybe companies are not created to satisfy their employees and care for their well-being, but when up to 90% of employees are dissatisfied with this kind of work environment, shouldn't companies listen to them instead of just doing another employee satisfaction survey, and then wondering why so many people in the company are so cynical about these surveys?

Even if a company's leaders don't place employee satisfaction high on the list of strategic priorities, **shouldn't they at least have the employees' intellectual productivity, engagement and creativity as a top priority?** Shouldn't they be interested in creating a social and physical working environment to realize optimal intellectual productivity?

Why don't architects inform their clients about the negative aspects of their choices?

To understand this state of affairs, let's go back to the beginning of the 20th century when modern building materials like steel-reinforced concrete, industrial steel and plate glass were fully developed.

As the big architects of that time, such as Mies van der Rohe and Le Corbusier, mastered these materials, they started to create huge open spaces. Their model, interestingly enough, was the huge open space of the factory hall from the 19th century.

When building high-rise office buildings it was now technically possible to imitate these huge halls on every single floor and to create free-flowing, adaptable, open spaces with only a minimum of walls or pillars.

They did this because it was technically possible, daring and new and because they fell in love with these open spaces; they did not create such office buildings because they were the ideal working environment for the people who had to work there.

> *"Architects built open offices because it became technically possible, not because it was good for the workers."*

This happened in parallel with the evolution from manual work to brainwork. Modern companies needed more and more offices. The huge open spaces the architects were able to build made it possible to design open offices where up to a hundred office workers could do routine work, while easily begin supervised by one manager. The non-routine brainwork was done by managers in their personal offices.

Little by little computers took over the routine brainwork and more and more people, not only managers, needed to do non-routine brainwork.

Knowledge work, work that needs reading, analysis, understanding and reflection, became the norm.

Companies realized that higher-level brainwork needed a level of attention and concentration that couldn't be found in the open-space office ... and so the cubicle was born.

To enhance informal contact, communication, sharing of information, creativity, collaboration, cohesion and culture; modern companies also needed to encourage face-to-face interaction, including of an informal and impromptu nature. They had the impression that the cubicles (of the Dilbert world) became islands and got in the way of free-floating ideas and the creativity needed to stay at the forefront of developments.

They skipped thinking more deeply about the root causes of the lack of communication or brainstorming with their architects about more creative solutions to resolve the communication problem. Probably they were also too much motivated by cost-cutting exercises by reducing the footprint of employees. As a result most companies just lowered the walls around cubicles or went back to the open-plan offices of the previous century where people were doing routine work that computers do now. They forgot that the work done by office workers had fundamentally changed and had become not more but much less routine.

> *"Basically the modern open plan office is not new nor future oriented, but a return to the past with modern materials."*

Many years ago a director at a TV broadcasting company asked me to participate in a program. Their new office building had been published in architecture magazines all over the world. Because I always had an interest in art in general and architecture specifically, instead of having him come to my house, I said that I'd prefer to come and visit his office. His reply surprised me: "Oh, no, no, I'd rather come to your house because we can't work in that new office". When I insisted I wanted to visit the building, he said "OK. I'll show you the building, but let's then have our meeting in the bistro a little further down the road". I was puzzled, but while visiting this very modern, award-wining building, I quickly realized that it was indeed unquestionably unfit for brainwork. The privacy, and especially the acoustical privacy, in the huge open office was zero and made worse by a high level of reverberation. People tried to cope with the situation by putting up cupboards (old ones, from the old offices, which did not fit in aesthetically at all), wearing headphones, gluing rubber foam to cupboards and walls, improvising cubicle walls with rubber foam they had brought from home etc. and we ended up having our meeting in the bistro.

How is it possible that companies and architects keep building offices that are (sometimes) aesthetically pleasing, if not exciting, but totally unfit for brainwork that needs concentration... to the extent that the brainworkers escape to a bistro (!?) for a quieter place to do their brainwork.

In one of the high-tech companies I worked with, a lawyer had to carefully double-check all contracts valued between 500,000 and 2 million Euros. He had to do this work in an open plan office, actually an old warehouse, where 25 other people were working, chatting and making phone calls. The effort needed to concentrate demanded so much energy that every evening he came home exhausted. When he did the same work from home, he could do much more work, making fewer mistakes and without feeling exhausted.

Isn't it strange that we build offices for brainworkers that exhaust them and cause them to make **more** mistakes, even to the extent that, as is the case in this example, just one of these mistakes might wipe out the entire cost cutting realized by choosing the cheapest office solution?

A global industrial company invited me to give a few stress management workshops because they suffered a high turnover amongst their account managers. I discovered that two years earlier, these 25 employees had been moved to an open office. Of course, the proclaimed reason to put them together in one room was to improve contact and the exchange of information. Many of these, mostly young people, complained that it was utterly impossible to do serious work or to have serious conversations in this noisy office. The management did not appreciate their feedback on the new offices at all. One day they even tried to make their point in a playful way by putting on motorbike helmets while working in that office. Management was not amused at all.

Then more and more clients complained that the new set-up ruined the conference calls. We all know how the background noise of one caller ruins the call for everybody. Since "we put our customers first"… finally management paid attention, took action and … installed a few telephone booths on the sides of the open space! A real story that looks as if it came straight from the world of Dilbert. The next thing that happened was that the employees started using the booths for any work requiring focus.

Why do companies keep opting for ill-conceived open offices when they are so detrimental to the stress-balance of the employees and the quality and quantity of their brainwork?

I think that we are dealing with a collusion of managers and architects who both have no clue about the fundamental genetic psychological needs of their brainworkers.

> *"Bad offices are still being built or rented, because of a collusion of managers and architects who both have no clue about the fundamental innate psychological needs of their brainworkers."*

Architects think in terms of aesthetics, space, imagination and originality. That is what the best ones get their assignments and international rewards for.

The bad ones just follow the managers' demands and cram in as many people as possible into un-aesthetic boxes that are as small and cheap as possible.

Both, however, too often do not consider the needs of the modern brainworkers.

When I ran this idea by junior and senior architects, I discovered that they had not learned anything about the physical, psychological and social impact of office design on employees. The junior architects even escape the creative (?), bustling bullpen of their own architectural firm and work from home when they need to reflect or focus on important or detailed work.

Sometimes the executives want on office building with the most daring architectural esthetical impact on the outside world. As the emperors, kings and popes of the past, they want a monument. This often is more related to the need of their egos and marketing than to the needs of their employees.

Architects love this and therefore collude with executives. There are very few who are knowledgeable enough about the innate needs of people and who are able to combine fantastic aesthetics with an excellent human environment.

Some choose not to contradict the executives when they discover that the demands are emotional rather than rational.

A chilling example is where Mark Zuckerberg and the world-class architect Frank Gehry look at a scale model of the new Facebook-office. Zuckerman says *"The idea is to make the perfect engineering space: one giant room that fits thousands of people, all close enough to collaborate together. It will be the largest open floor plan in the world ... "* and the architect does not react[60]. Of course not, if you are chosen to build a 5 billion $ office, you try to realize the CEO's dream, even if you know it's a nightmare (or could it be that the architect really doesn't know?).

Zuckerberg and co use the most modern neuropsychological and sociological research and algorithms to make Facebook products as addictive as possible (without any concern about its consequences for the users, especially children and society). Why does he ignore the decades of neuro-psycho-sociological research about the negative impact of open space offices on people? Or doesn't he know? Then the question is why he never asked his gifted researchers to check his ideas against the research.

Maybe, in the antisocial-media companies, the open offices played a role in preventing employees from thinking ahead, broad and deep about their business model and to reflect on the very negative impact of their products and their company on their users, on children, on society. Luckily, some of them got a wake-up call when they saw the impact on their own children[61].

Another unsettling statement about open offices is from an architect interviewed by the researcher Rachel Hirst[62] about an open office she studied. He said: "I think it's like going to a nudist beach. You know, first you're a little bit worried that everyone's looking at you, but then you think, hang on, everybody else is naked, no one's looking at each other, I think that's what'll happen, they'll get on with it.".

What a flabbergasting lack of elementary knowledge about and disrespect for human beings. Hirst continues correctly "The only problem is that sociological research of nudist beaches has shown that people do continue to watch each other–men in particular, often in groups, look obsessively at women," And exactly the same thing happens in open offices ánd especially towards women. As you read in the quote in the second chapter of this text: most people do NOT adapt over time, but suffer.

The mistake so many executives as well as professionals make is that they think that because something is technically possible, it's better. In fact a fancy new technological solution can be (much) worse.

This is not only true for always being connected, which has a very negative impact on intellectual productivity, creativity and stress. It also is true for hot-desking, clean desks, huge open office spaces, taking notes on a tablet instead of on paper etc...

Hot-desking in combination with clean-desking as a solution to use office space more "rationally" is an excellent example amongst many. Hot-desking is possible thanks to technical solutions like mobile phones and omnipresent fast Ethernet or Wi-Fi connections. But that does not mean it is a good solution. In most cases this solution is worse than the problem, because it does not take into account the very basic, innate needs of human beings I described above. It's even worse when companies do not allow personalization of the workplace with pictures, diplomas, souvenirs etc.

Moreover when employees arrive at a clean-desks it costs a lot more time to dive back into the work they were doing and to build up concentration. Moreover, a messy desk may promote creative thinking and stimulate novel ideas, unconventional choices less confirmatory information processing[63].

> *"If a cluttered desk is a sign of a cluttered mind, of what, then, is an empty desk a sign?"*

Albert Einstein[3]

Hence, you should test out any hype of a "new way of working" in a carefully designed pilot with excellent before and after action reviews, or you need to check the existing research, especially when tech companies try to sell you their gadgets and "solutions".

From an internationally renowned, very senior architect I learned:

1. *That building a good open and flexible office is not cheaper than building individual offices. It is actually more expensive among other things because of the high costs of noise elimination and the high degree of customization needed to the different kinds of work people do.*

2. *That offices being built in recent years are even worse than before, because most companies don't build offices that are custom-made for the needs of their own employees and the specificities of their work. They lease offices from project developers who have only one goal in mind: to build offices as cheaply as possible in order to earn as high a margin as possible, with no interest whatsoever for the poor workers who will have to work in them.*

So for both managers and architects, the main reason why they keep building these brain-warehouses seems to be lack of knowledge.

---

3 Probably apocryphal. I could not find the exact reference.

If you talk to employees about the issue, they are much more cynical about the reasons why a particular office lay-out was chosen. Some see the open offices as a clear sign of mistrust of the company, with managers who want to be able to check all the time on what their employees are doing.

The great majority, however, see their offices as the cheapest possible solution and they resent that leadership teams ignore there wishes and complaints.

> *"Our management is of the 'listen to my words but do not look at my deeds' kind. Look at these posters: we are declared to be our company's most valued asset. However, when you look at our offices, you see we are treated like ****ing cattle. Or to put it politely, we are certainly not treated like the most valued asset".*

Employees' cynicism is fed by the fact that when they look at the offices of their (senior) managers, they often see a maximum of privacy and a minimum of noise. This raises questions in their minds: Are their managers the only ones who need to concentrate to make the best use of their brains? Do all the other employees only do routine brainwork? Is spontaneous interaction and communication not important for senior managers?

Employees often understand very well that the gain from the cheapest building is immediate and easy to demonstrate in building and maintenance costs, while the pain is long term and more difficult to calculate in terms of revenue losses and a lower quality and quantity of intellectual productivity.

Why do companies still invest billions in new office buildings

Why do CEO's of the biggest tech companies invest billions in new office buildings to begin with, when they hyped the concept of employees as "free agents" working anytime, anywhere?

The reason why the free-agent idea does not work and that companies need good offices, is that the "free agent" is a romantic urban myth linked to that of the free cowboy roaming the prairies, riding from farm to farm, while on his way fighting the Indians. Only a very small minority of employees are happy with that free agent role. That's certainly true for most free agents in the gig-economy, who cannot find steady work, and who work for anybody, anytime, anywhere for fees that often do not allow a decent living.

The heart of the matter is that humans are social animals, with a genetic need to belong to a tribe. Therefore a company can only be sustainably successful if it succeeds as a social organization. So even top-tech companies still build offices although most work can be done remotely, because they learned, sometimes the hard way, that they need to build social relations where people get a feeling of belonging and where they can plug their brains into the brains of their colleagues. It turns out that contact via the most sophisticated technology is still a poor substitute for a good live conversation.

A badly designed open office, however, can jeopardize the social organization you need to be successful.

CONCLUSION:
Open offices, closed brains.

Most open offices are a disaster for brainworkers' intellectual productivity. They should be called brain-jails, places to chain and lock away intellectual productivity and creativity. The most detrimental factor is a lack of privacy and above all the lack of acoustic privacy.

Even in companies where the rhetoric of executives about improved communication, collaboration and flexibility is sincere, many (very) bad offices are still being built. Why? Because the executives responsible for the buildings, as well as their architects, have no knowledge of the fundamental needs of brainworkers and their brains. They do not realize that the priority should be privacy in order to enable concentration and that without this privacy it is impossible to improve collaboration and communication.

"When collaboration and communication need improvement, start thinking about the management culture, not about the office walls."

In fact, when collaboration and communication need to be improved, office walls are the last place to look for a solution. The main walls hindering communication and collaboration are in your culture and, first and foremost, your management culture. No removal or lowering of office and cubicle walls will change that. On the contrary, if your management communication and collaboration culture is poor, the rhetoric about the need for cheap, open offices to improve collaboration will only raise the cynicism and lower the motivation. If your communication and collaboration culture is good, no walls will stop it.

Similarly, even excellent "flexible" offices will not make a rigid company more flexible because that rigidity is the result of a wider company culture, and that culture is for the most part determined by the leadership culture. In comparison with the huge impact of leadership style, office layout pales into insignificance

SOLUTIONS: Focus first

In my book "BrainChains" I describe the tools, tips and tricks that can improve your intellectual productivity at three levels, and I'll keep this same approach here for the Fifth BrainChain:

1. **The ME-level**: *What can I do to improve the quality and quantity of my brainwork.*

2. **The WE-level**: *These are things you can do with colleagues and peers. For managers, there are two more WEs: things you can do with your team for the part of the business you are responsible for; and initiatives you can take in your boss's team.*

3. **The THEY-level**: *This is about what people higher up in the hierarchy can and should do to improve brainwork in the organization as a whole or in the part they are responsible for.*

For the Fifth BrainChain the main responsibility lies at the 'They' level and so I understand that my suggestions for the two other levels may feel like a Band-Aid where major surgery is needed.

Please email me if you know of other creative solutions at any of these levels at office@compernolle.com.

At the "Me" level

Fight bad offices at work

A few examples of tools people use when they need to concentrate on high value-added, difficult brainwork in an open office such as:

- Creating a make-shift movable cubicle or dividing wall from cardboard and foam rubber, ideally after discussing the idea with the people around you and inviting them to join your effort to improve intellectual productivity and reduce exhaustion (I found an interesting portable solution designed by Kawamura & Ganjavian[64]);

- Putting up a DO NOT DISTURB sign or better a sign saying: "Please do not disturb. At 11 I am available for any questions", while putting the same message on your voice-mail and out of office message.

- Finding a seldom used quiet office or corner somewhere else in the building.

- If there is no way to escape the distractions at work, some people fly to their home or a coffee-bar in the neighbourhood.

- Since noise is the number one distractor, you might consider wearing noise-cancelling headphones or motorbike helmets or using wax earplugs.

If you want to buy earplugs or headsets, have a look at the different characteristics of solutions going from ultra cheap ear-plugs to very expensive headphones at http://www.noisehelp.com/noise-protection.html and http://www.audiocheck.net/earplugreviews_index.php, where I learned that some cheap wax-cotton earplugs are the best solution to block noise, even better than the passive noise-isolating ear canal headphones and the expensive noise-cancellation headphones.

It's also worth noting that headsets have the additional advantage that they give a clear signal: "Do not disturb!". Hence, some people people use big old headphones that even don't work anymore.

For some people "white noise", "pink noise" or "grey noise" helps them to concentrate by masking other background noises[65] . Some people put it on their headphones. Others are angry enough to put it on their speakers in their cubicle... if they still have the luxury of a cubicle.

However, it is very difficult to get masking-noise right because the frequencies as we consciously perceive them have a complicated relationship with the frequencies at the source. Experiments have been done with white noise, pink noise and grey noise. The evidence suggests that grey noise most closely matches the way our ear deals with the different frequencies.

Secondly, the effect of masking noise also depends on the quality of our hearing. Older people whose hearing has naturally deteriorated with age or young people who have ruined their hearing with an overdose of decibels from earphones or loudspeakers at festivals need a different masking sound than people with perfect hearing.

A third problem with masking sound is that its usefulness depends on the loudness of the sound being masked. This changes all the time, alternating with silent periods.

Hence a level of masking-noise that is useful when there is a lot of office noise itself becomes an annoyance when the office is quiet. As a result, systems that adapt to the level of office noise are being developed.

Last but not least, there are also important individual perceptual differences. What is a good masking-noise for one person is an unbearable noise for somebody else. Introverts perform better than extroverts when there is no background noise or music at all.

In general both perform worse with noise, but the introverts more so than the extraverts[66]. Some extraverts do even better with some distraction noise or music than without, especially when the task is boring.[67]

If you want to experiment yourself with masking-noise, try it out at http://mynoise.net/NoiseMachines/whiteNoiseGenerator.php. Here you can even make your own custom-made masking-noise based on the quality of your hearing and the noise in your working environment. If you find a good masking-noise, you can put it on your headphones or speakers.

In any case, the conclusion is that masking-noise is certainly no panacea for resolving the noise problems of a badly designed office.

Too many employees think about these kind of solutions but don't dare use them because they fear it will be considered anti-social. The interesting thing is that when I push my audiences to openly discuss this with their peers, they usually find out that many, if not most, of them suffer from noise pollution but don't dare use headphones. They then collude and start using them as a group.

Beyond these makeshift tools, the best solution of course is convincing your employer of how counter-productive your offices are or organizing a revolt of the brainworkers, as the manual workers of the first industrial revolution did when they revolted against their working environments and managed to change them. To help you, I do not demand copyrights on this booklet. You may distribute it freely, as a whole or in parts, as long as you credit my work by mentioning the source as: *"How To Design Brain-Friendly Offices" by Theo Compernolle. MD., PhD. Compublications* www.brainchains.info.

If approaching the managers responsible for your office directly does not work, you can also try a more subversive approach by "forgetting" copies or extracts of this book near photocopiers, coffee machines or water coolers or by adding it "by accident" as an attachment to an email sent to many large groups of employees. Just be creative.

If you belong to Generation Y or later, you may love the lively, animated, entertaining atmosphere of an open office. You may be convinced that it does not hinder your intellectual productivity and creativity. However, think twice, because as I describe in "BrainChains" and "How To Unchain Your Brain", all the research proves you dead wrong.

Avoid reflection killers when you work at home too

Given the chance, more and more brainworkers avoid the office by working at home. This is not only because this flexibility has other advantages but also because many modern offices are totally unfit for difficult or complex intellectual work.

When you work from home, don't forget: home is a soft emotional, relational culture, while work is a hard, contractual one. At home, you don't have bosses, contracts, appointments, calendars, bonuses and sanctions. If there are no clear boundaries, if you mix both without making deliberate choices, the "hard" work will win in terms of time and the "soft" home will interfere emotionally. This is very evident in my work with families with a family business[68].

Do not try to combine household, family and work; everything will suffer from it. When you work from home, family, friends, children, pets and acquaintances will often not consider this real work and will think you can be disturbed at any time. Explain the situation to them, set rules and stick to them.

It is important to pay attention to the way you organize yourself when working from home.

In the beginning of this "new way of working" movement the most intelligent companies made a real effort to help and advise their employees to set up proper home offices.

Now working at home has become so "normal" that many companies don't even think about assisting their flexible workforce in organizing work at home.

Therefore, when you work at home, organize yourself so that you can focus. Don't underestimate the impact your working environment has on the quality of your work and on your focus.

Get a proper desk and work in a room with the fewest possible disturbances. Invest in it: look at a specialist office store.

Spoil yourself: get a good desk, an excellent chair and a very large computer screen in the quietest room with a nice view.

You will spend many hours there, so make it comfortable.

Read the chapter about "Local Stress" in "BrainChains", where I explain that once you experience pain because of bad ergonomics at home, it's sometimes too late. At home too, masking-noise may help if you are disturbed by noise around you.

Keep to a time schedule. Set time for email, phone calls, household chores and breaks. **The secret to your intellectual productivity is, at home as in the office, is batch-processing,** an idea that I describe in "BrainChains" and "How To Unchain Your Brain".

**You loose all rights to complain
about your open office
if you are an always connected
multitasker!**

Most important of all: earmark undisturbed focus time to work on important tasks **without any interruptions**, with your email and phones switched off.

Above all, postpone all social media and web-surfing until after your work for the day is done. Do not use them as a break to relax. They are so addictive that again and again you will spend much more time with them than you planned. Especially because at home there is no longer any social control on the hours you spend online, while at work you might avoid being caught spending too much time with social media or web-surfing. It's better to use going online as a reward for a day of really hard and focused work... if you have nothing healthier to relax with.

Get dressed for work as the quality of your work will be better than if you stay in your pyjamas or jogging outfit.

By the way, no matter whether or not you are working in the living room, get the TV out of your view. Good intellectual work is incompatible with TV. If you think you are an exception, you are totally wrong and you should read "BrainChains".

At the "We" level: band together against badly designed offices

To help you open the discussion about an office that is being planned or about necessary improvements to an existing one, I have made this book about the negative influence of offices without copyrights. You can copy all you need for non-commercial use, as long as you mention the source as: *"How To Design Brain-Friendly Offices" by Theo Compernolle. MD., PhD. Compublications* www.brainchains. info. Free copies of older versions of this book are available on www.brainchains.com.

At the "They" level: a new office is a strategic change project, not a building project.

Building, leasing or redesigning a new office is not a building project, but a change project with optimizing the intellectual productivity as its goal. Therefore the needs of the brainworkers are central and strengthening their focus is the first priority.

A strategic change project focussing on the needs of brainworkers and their brains

Most executives involved in building, leasing or redesigning an office, see it as an architectural, material project, while in fact it is a huge, difficult and strategic change project. It is a people project affecting the company culture, the hearts, the minds, the productivity and the wellbeing of the employees. Underestimating the strategic change aspect is a costly mistake. Managing a change of offices as a strategic change project is a necessary requirement for success.

When you do manage it as a change project, keep in mind that 70% of change projects, big and small, fail to deliver because they neglect the "soft", the human aspects of change. Badly managed they provoke unnecessary resistance and loss of motivation.

One of the often neglected aspects is engaging the office workers in the design process in a continuous exchange of information in two directions. Too often the office is designed by executives and specialists and then imposed on the users.

The architect I mentioned before, comparing an open office with a nudist beach to which the users just have to get used to, is a blatant example.

Moreover, many offices and "new ways of working" are developed by executives and architects from one culture. They are then callously imposed on people in other countries without taking into account to what extent they may go against deep-rooted cultural difference and consequently undermine the intellectual productivity and collaboration.

The subject of how to run a successful change project is one I am very interested in, but it's beyond the scope of this book.

Another aspect it has in common with all big change projects is that you can never get it right from the start. It always is a process of trial and error, of continuous improvement in a continuous feedback-loop between executives and office workers. An office is not a monument, but a living work environment continuously adapting to the needs of the people. Therefore, to succeed you need flexible managers, flexible people and a flexible building. The task of the facilities manager is not to keep the building in its original pristine condition, but to continuously adapt it to the needs of the people.

To play it safe, especially in internationally operating companies, it often is wise to start with one or two pilot projects, with careful before action reviews and after action reviews.

The executives of global company decided to start with two pilot offices on two continents, to test out there ideas about the new way of working and the concept of the new offices they developed for this. The two offices were exactly the same in design. One of the features they had were cubicles designed for non-confidential phone calls. They were well insulated so that the noise of the phone calls would not disturb the other workers in the open offices.

In both offices management discovered that people tried to come early to occupy the cubicles for their regular work.

In one office management reacted with "You are not following the rules. Please leave the cubicle when you are not making a phone call"

In the Asian office, the manager realised that probably the cubicles fulfilled unmet needs of the workers. She opened the discussion and found out that the open offices were too noisy to concentrate, not only because of the conversations and phone calls, but also because of the noise of the foosball table and the pantry. As a result, following the priorities of the workers, they decided to transform the lounge space into a library space with desks and monitors, where people were not allowed to talk or phone.

In the discussion I later had with them, they realised that it would even be better to completely reverse their priorities and turn the whole open space into a library, with plenty of boots and cubicles for noisy work, while insulating the pantry and moving the foosball to the income hall.

In this company, the workers and the buildings were flexible, but the managers in the first office were not.

Theoretically, there are two paths to follow when building or renovating an office.

The first path is to see the office (and the employees) as a cost and demand that employees adapt to a workspace designed for short-term cost-efficiency. This is actually what too many companies do.

This will not work because it took our inner savannah-dweller hundreds of thousands of years to evolve to what (s)he is today. It is ridiculous to think that the way our brain and the rest of our body functions evolved over hundreds of thousands of years can adapt in a few decades to an unfit work environment.

If people try to adapt to a bad office, they might succeed to some extent, but the continuous neglect of the funda-mental needs of the inner savannah-dweller will cause a lot of chronic stress, exhaustion, dissatisfaction and a deterioration in performance.

The only alternative, to paraphrase Schopenhauer, is to stop hiring the best and the brightest brains and instead look for the the brains that can best handle the interruptions of open offices...because there is nothing to interrupt.

> *"Too many flexible offices demand a lot of flexibility from the workers who have to adapt to the office instead of the other way around."*

The second path is to see the building or leasing of an office as an investment in people, to optimize the employees' intellectual productivity and adapt the workplace to the very fundamental needs of the brainworkers and their inner savannah-dweller.

The solution: a flexible office were privacy is guaranteed and contact inescapable

There is a solution for designing flexible offices that maximize intellectual productivity by eliminating distractions and enhancing collaboration, but it rarely gets a chance to be implemented.

First of all because it is expensive and too many executives do not realize that cutting the cost of peanuts is always peanuts, while the slightest improvement in productivity is gold in the coffers.

Secondly because it requires a degree of flexibility that the management of many companies do not have.

And thirdly because it calls for an interest in the different needs of different workers.

The solution is called the flexible office. You may well be thinking right now, "That's not a solution... No way... I work in one of those, it's a disaster...!!!".

It is not a real flexible office flexible office if it demands a lot of flexibility from the workers who have to adapt to the office instead of the other way around.

If you are really concerned about improving intellectual productivity, don't be put off by what seems to be an unsolvable dilemma: high quality brainwork needs high privacy, interaction needs low privacy. This is only a dilemma if you try to realize it in the same space. **You should not try to combine focus and contact in one and the same space, but combine them in different spaces or subspaces.**

However, you should tackle this challenge the other way around from how it's usually approached. Your priority should not be contact and communication.

Your top priority should be to guarantee the brainworkers the optimal privacy that their thinking-brain needs when they are doing their solitary high-level brainwork.

This is the most neglected, the most difficult and the most expensive part.

Since all solo brainwork, except routine work, needs focus, the individual workspaces should provide an optimal level of privacy, eliminating all unwanted intrusions.

Only when that is guaranteed should you start looking for ways to increase collaboration and communication, without sacrificing employees' ability to focus.

Only when the focus is guaranteed can you make the building encourage, if not force, people to interact as soon as they leave their thinking bubble.

Don't forget that a lack of privacy often decreases meaningful communication and collaboration.

Flexible enough to adapt to different tasks
Since the tasks of modern brainworkers are as varied as their needs, offices should above all be flexible so that

people can have the degree of privacy they need to be optimally productive at that moment for that particular task.

In the table below I tried to summarize the most important functions an office has to fulfil and the corresponding needs of the brainworkers that have to be satisfied.

Basically the dilemma is resolved by providing a very flexible mix of workspaces, flexible in the sense that the offices flexibly adapt to the needs of the workers and their work instead of the other (and more usual) way around.

Functions of a flexible office: FOCUS FIRST

	Tasks	Needs	Facilities
Reflection Concentration	Focused individual intellectual work, reflection	Sensory Privacy Quiet (!), light, familiar, personal stuff at hand.	Visual/acoustical shielded from all the other activities, windows, easy to personalize
Communication	Actual or virtual communication = joint reflection	No distraction Visual / auditory protection	Acoustically (and visually) shielded
Collaboration	Group meetings, discussions, presentations, virtual conferences, brainstorming	Stimulating, room, light,	Space, windows, good acoustics, tools, technology, not disturbing others
Restoration	Time out: relax and recuperate or move about	Or quiet → Or interactive → Or active →	→"meditation room" →"pantry-lounge" →"fitness"

Priority: protect concentrated reflection
Don't let the other tasks disturb people's focus.

I have visited a few correctly designed offices that have found a solution for the contact-focus dilemma. In most, however, the starting point was wrong by giving top priority to "being together", exchanging information and collaboration while putting privacy and concentration second. The lack of attention paid to noise and other disruptions was obvious. The workers were sitting in a busy marketplace, but had the possibility to escape to a few more quiet rooms when they needed to concentrate.

A rather simple improvement was to reverse the priorities and to change the busy marketplace into a library environment. Usually this needed some retrofitting to eliminate noise. Although eliminating noise can be difficult and expensive, the most difficult part often is to change the social rules.

At the start some people may even resist the change,

- Because they never had the experience of the power of prolonged concentration,

- Because they prefer the fun,

- Because they cannot postpone the gratification of getting or giving an answer immediately,

- Because they suffer FOMO (fear of missing out) or FOBE (fear of being excluded)[4],

- Because they experience longer periods of concentration as boring etc.

Managers who realize that this is a major change and who manage it as a strategic change-project, play an important role to motivate the employees to continue the new way of working until they discover the advantages for themselves.

The very creative CEO of a small but fast growing company, after reading BrainChains, introduced a focus oriented new way of working as a parlor game "Do not disturb". People were asked to move each other's pawn back or forth on the "Do not disturb" game board, depending on how each worker followed the "do not disturb" rules. Each week, the winner got a voucher for a wellness activity, the loser had to bring a self-made caked to share.

One of the rules was that three times a day, during forty-five minutes, nobody was allowed to disturb anybody else. These hours were called "Do Not Disturb Time". Initially many em-

---

4 Further explained in "BrainChains"

ployees did not like the idea, they preferred to ask their question or give their comments anytime immediately. The CEO convinced them not to stop, but to see it as an experiment.

After six weeks, everybody was so convinced of the positive impact of the "Do Not Disturb Time" on their productivity and wellbeing that they decided themselves to add a fourth "Do Not Disturb" period.

Because they enjoyed the positive impact on their brainwork so much, they started calling these distraction-free periods a feast for our brains and "Brain-parties" and later it became a custom to light up the garlands of colourful lightbulbs, they used for birthday parties, at the beginning of each Brain-party giving everybody a clear signal "don't disturb".

The positive impact of less distractions on their work, then motivated them to develop a playful method to regain control of their powerful personal distractor: their smartphone. Once all technology was eliminated form their meetings, the meeting became much shorter, sometimes only lasting 15 minutes instead of an hour.

The result of the project was a very significant increase in productivity, so much so that notwithstanding a significant increase in workload, everybody finishes their jobs within the regular office hours and spent more time with their families. This now is a competitive advantage in the war for talent against much bigger companies"

Flexible enough to adapt to different needs
What the right office is for an employee, not only depends on the task but also on personality types.

Just one example. In "BrainChains" I describe how introverts and extroverts for instance have often different needs. Take the example of noise, which has such a negative impact, even when people are not aware of it. The more introverted people, who are more acutely aware of

noise and its effects, should not only be given ample pos-
sibilities to find a quiet space, but also they should not be
treated like fussy weaklings but be valued as the thorough
thinkers they are and as the canaries in the coalmine who
give the early warning signals about an unhealthy working
environment. If you value their deep thinking, way not
give them a private or small shared office?

Since a high degree of personalization (the possibility to
mark a personal territory with pictures, souvenirs, awards
etc.) helps people to concentrate and protects them to
some extent against the exhaustion caused by low privacy,
employees should be allowed, if not actively encouraged,
to personalize their workspace. Female employees are
often more acutely aware of this positive impact, so we
should not only give them the room to do this, but also
use their signal to encourage everybody to do so.

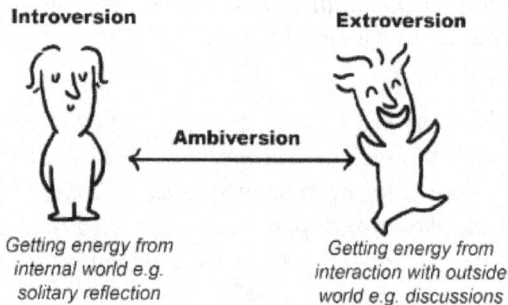

Introversion

Extroversion

Ambiversion

Getting energy from
internal world e.g.
solitary reflection

Getting energy from
interaction with outside
world e.g. discussions

While visiting offices in many different companies I often
wondered: Why don't they let employees choose the space
that is most comfortable for them. Different personalities
will choose vastly different locations and even work spaces.
If somebody prefers a quiet solo-office for her solo-work,
why not let her use one. If another person prefers a higher
cubicle wall or a different chair or desk, why not let him
have it. If a team would like much more plants, let them

bring them and care for them themselves. The cost is peanuts compared to the productivity gains of a happy worker. Modern technology allows companies to customize their products for very specific needs of their customers. The technology also allow companies to customize the work environment to the needs of their workers. Why doesn't it happen?

The needs of one group of people is a particular challenge.

As I described above many young people who are hyper-connected from their childhood on, multitask all the time and not only allow but actively search for continuous distraction.

Despite all the evidence to the contrary, they are convinced that they can multitask and task-switch without negative consequences for their cognitive performance; in fact the negative impact is substantial.

Nor do they realize that they have greater difficulties focusing and concentrating in order to reflect, than people who multitask less. It is therefore possible that they might prefer a bustling, open office despite the negative impact on their intellectual productivity.

Stop the noise

The number one intrusion that kills intellectual productivity is noise. When you think about privacy, noise elimination should be your top priority because noise has an extremely negative impact on intellectual productivity, satisfaction, motivation and increases emotional exhaustion.

Within that category, the worst are intelligible conversations, and within this category the most awful are phone conversations.

Fight noise on all fronts: the height and acoustic absorption quality of the floors, ceilings and walls, the degree of reverberation (glass and bare walls!), and the height and acoustic absorption quality of the (cubicle) walls. The first rule of thumb is simple: open offices + flat hard surfaces = bad news for productivity. Noise reduction is never cheap, especially to retrofit a badly built office because so many interacting variables have to be addressed, but it is always worth the investment. Provide an easy escape to separate rooms where people can have phone calls or conversations without bothering others.

As I explained in section two, just applying some masking-noise, in particular to mask speech, is not going to do the job. On the contrary, since the effect of the masker depends on the task at hand, the personality and hearing of the employee, it will improve the situation for some and drive many others crazy.

> *Open offices + flat hard surfaces*
> *= low productivity.*

Encourage people to be polite and stimulate groups to develop their rules of engagement. The loudness and frequency with which they speak will make a big difference. They all should know about the Lombard effect and react against the spontaneous tendency to speak louder when there is background noise.

The problem is that there is often no alternative place to go and since disruptive, uncontrollable noise tends to increase aggression, courtesy will be an early victim.

Of course there are other physical aspects of a building that can be improved. For example the ones I described in the chapter "Offices that abuse our inner savannah dweller". We could, for example, discuss the research about the different impact of different colours, the height of the space, providing ample water and fruit. However, not only the research about these factors has more ambiguous results, but none of them have as big a positive impact as privacy and silence, maybe with one exception: ample daylight, as you probably have discovered reading the table "Functions of a Flexible Office" above. People with a window view are more productive, even in a call centre.

A thinking framework to realise an excellent flexible office.
In the figure below, you find a model that I made to summarize what I have learned from my research. Beware! This is a thinking framework, a representation of different solutions that a flexible office has to provide for different aspects of brainwork and different types of people. *It is not an actual floor plan*[69]. For example, if the contact spaces are too far away from the focus spaces, especially when they are on another floor, people will not use them and will continue to disturb others by having discussions. On the other hand, the closer the contact-spaces are to the focus-spaces, the more difficult and expensive it will be to achieve the necessary acoustic and visual privacy.

All the different spaces can even be in one open office as long as concentration gets the first priority by eliminating noise and optimizing privacy.

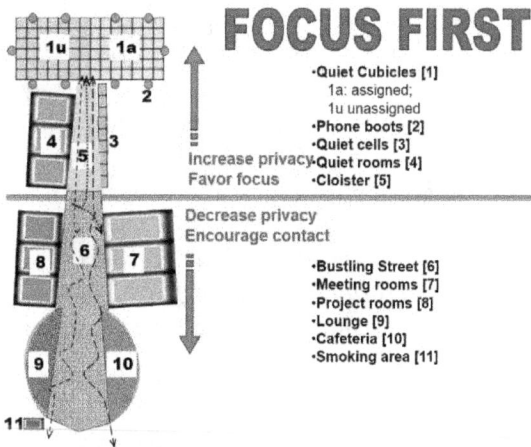

FOCUS FIRST

·**Quiet Cubicles [1]**
  1a: assigned;
  1u unassigned
·**Phone boots [2]**
·**Quiet cells [3]**
Increase privacy ·**Quiet rooms [4]**
Favor focus ·**Cloister [5]**

Decrease privacy
Encourage contact

·**Bustling Street [6]**
·**Meeting rooms [7]**
·**Project rooms [8]**
·**Lounge [9]**
·**Cafeteria [10]**
·**Smoking area [11]**

The most important message of the model is that for a flexible open office focus/privacy should be the FIRST priority and NOT communication or other goals like cost cutting.

So what we need in a brainwork-enhancing flexible (open) office are quiet cubicles or at the very least very quiet workplaces in an open zone where the social rules create a *"library atmosphere"* [1]. Some desks are *assigned* to people who spend lots of time in the office doing solo brainwork. These people get the first choice to have their own cubicle or desk and they should be allowed, if not stimulated, to personalize their desk. If you want to frustrate them to the level of desperation, let those people hot-desk too. You should avoid hot-desking/clean-desking as much as possible anyway, because it ignores too many innate needs of people.

It is not because a cubicle or a desk-space is not used for several hours of the day that keeping it reserved for the absent worker is a waste of space and money. It is an investment in a little superfluous space to get the best possible brainwork, productivity, creativity and wellbeing.

It's not because hot-desking combined with clean-desking is technically possible and cheaper that it is better, on the contrary. Too many extreme lean rationalizations of office use are totally irrational because they do not take into account the directions for use of human beings. Therefore, hot-desking with clean-desking is most often a little penny-wise, but very pound-foolish.

> *"Too many extreme lean rationalizations of office use are totally irrational, because they do not take into account the directions for use of human beings."*

There are also *unassigned* cubicles or desks for people who spend less time in the office. In these cubicles too, acoustic, visual, olfactory and sensorial intrusions are eliminated.

Everybody should also learn to *respect "do not disturb" signs* as long as they mention when the no-disturbance period ends. In many offices, organising "do not disturb" periods several times a day are easy to organize.

Ideally, part of this privacy should also be that the brain-workers can *control, at least a little, the level of light and temperature*. An individual adjustable lamp is easy.

Personal temperature control seems impossible, but when I started thinking about this I wondered if that is really the case, because it doesn't require anything more than the individual temperature controls, or at least air-flow adjustment controls, provided for different seats in a car or plane.

To keep the open zone or cubicle zone quiet and especially to eliminate demilogues, people should leave their cubicles and go to *telephone booths* [2] for telephone conversations or to *quiet cells* [3] for any conversation or discussion.

This is made easier in those companies where all fixed-line phones have already been eliminated and all employees use a mobile phone.

Forwarding a call to the phone in a quiet cell should not be too difficult, especially if people work on laptops with docking stations and can take their information with them. People can also use these quiet cells for brainwork or 1:1 conversations that need more privacy than an open office or cubicle can provide, if needed even for a prolonged time.

For people who do not like to work in a cubicle all by themselves, for example because they have more routine work, *quiet rooms* [4] are provided, shared by 2-4 people who keep their room basically quiet too by using telephone booths and quiet cells.

If continuous easy interactions are needed, for example in the creative brainstorm phase of a project, people can move together to a *project room* [8] and stay there for a particular phase of the project. From there they can always escape to an unassigned cubicle, a cell or even a quiet room, if they need to focus for part of their work, such as studying complex spreadsheets or working out the details of the implementation.

War-rooms for brainstorming and following big projects should certainly not follow the clean desk philosophy.

As I explained, clean-desks force people to lose time to build up concentration and get into the subject they were studying.

This is also true for project-rooms. The group should be allowed to leave all their flipcharts, stickers and posters permanently on the wall and stuff like models on the tables, so that when entering the room they are at once in the centre of the project, immediately focused on the task. It's not because a project-room or war-room is not used for big parts of the day, that you should see it as a waste of space. Tech companies try to sell all kinds of electronic gadgets to replace the "junk" spread all over project-rooms, here too it's not because it's technically possible that it is better. On the contrary. For project-rooms too, the possible gain of space and money via a "rationalization" of office-space by trying to avoid that project rooms are not used part of the day, is peanuts compared to the loss of intellectual productivity, creativity and wellbeing.

Further away in the non-privacy zone we find meeting rooms [7], a lounge area with a shared printing area [9], a cafeteria [10] and a smoking area [11], and why not have a covered outside area where non-smokers can relax and breathe some real, fresh air.

Without standing still,
you won't move ahead!

An important solution is "the street" or "market". As soon as employees leave their focus-bubbles they are on the street, a street they cannot avoid. The street has two very distinct parts: the cloister [5] and the bustling street [6].

Closer to the quiet zone, the street has the feeling of a monastery corridor with dimmer light, soft colours, carpets, no posters... helping everybody to become quiet and to start concentrating. It also is a buffer for the quiet zone against the noise of the bustling part.

Closer to the non-privacy areas, the street becomes broader, full of light, open, brightly coloured, attractive, stimulating, with changing posters and flat panel displays, product displays, coffee and water corners, fruit baskets etc. to stimulate bumping into each other, loitering, staying, meeting, talking and serendipitous encounters.

This kind of office is also a solution for the problem that different phases of a project or different tasks need a different kind of office. In the initial creative, brainstorming phase an office is needed where people share the same soundproof war-room - a pressure cooker - for many hours. In the next phase, or sometimes at the same time, they need moments of privacy to focus, to drill down into the details, to study all the information and the different options and to plan the implementation of the part they are responsible for.

This moving about during the work-day is also excellent for employees' physical condition. It will also stimulate them to better plan their work and in particular to ear-mark undisturbed time for reflection where they totally disconnect from email, phone and other interruptions and disturbances.

It is totally irrational or uninformed to think that, while a brainworker is joining a team in a meeting room or a project room for a few hours, her empty desk is a waste of space and should be left clean to be occupied by some-body else.

On the contrary, when she returns from the meeting room, she should have left all her "junk" on her desk, to dive at once in her part of the project.

When while working on her part and wondering about an aspect of the project, she must be able to go back to the project room, with all the "junk" laying around where the group left it, to quickly find the information she needs.

Moreover, as we discussed already, this junk, this clutter, this chaos stimulates creativity.

Of course, there are more things that are important for a healthy office, like the quality of the air conditioning, the electrical lighting etc…, but these are better known. There is one often forgotten aspect however, that has a significant impact on the intellectual productivity and creativity: **daylight**. I suffer from this neglect myself way too often when I have meetings and workshops with my clients. More often than not, meeting rooms have no windows to the outside world, while all (and I really mean all) rooms where people are supposed to be creative should have windows to the outside world, also and especially the meeting rooms[70].

Sergio Altomonte hits the bulls-eye in the conclusion of his excellent review of much of the available research: *"In the practice of design, daylighting should not be considered as an afterthought which is taken into account only when the spatial characters of the building have already taken shape. Rather, daylight should be valued as a necessity that literally drives and directs the design of a built environment from its early stages of conception and development, dictating the quality of internal spaces and ultimately leading to buildings which are economically cheaper to run, less harmful for the environment, and, above all, healthy, inspiring and stimulating for their occupants"*.

CONCLUSION: Put your brainworkers and the needs of their brains first, radically first.

Too often offices are built forgetting that in the last few decades office work has fundamentally changed from low-level routine work to higher-level knowledge work that needs focus, attention, concentration, abstraction, analysis, synthesis, creativity and thinking forward, deep and wide. This is work only a human brain can do because it is based on reflection, knowledge and insight.

The open offices that were kind of okay for the old routine work, are clearly a disaster for knowledge work.

Sometimes executives who really care about people, build or lease brain-hostile offices anyway, because they lack the necessary knowledge. It is also clear that they don't know that ill-conceived open offices often worsen rather than improve communication and collaboration.

When these offices are built by executives who prioritize cost cutting, the sad fact is that these buildings are not even penny-wise and are certainly very pound-foolish.

The solution is a flexible office, but not in the usual sense of office workers having to be very flexible to adapt to rigid counter-productive office buildings, which in fact results in lower intellectual productivity, frustration and exhaustion. A flexible building should, to the greatest extent possible, adapt to the needs of the workers and not the other way around.

When planning such an office, the first priority should be the brainworkers' privacy, meaning protection from any unwanted intrusions or interruptions via any of the senses. Of these, noise has the worst impact of all. Only when privacy is assured can initiatives to improve collaboration be successful.

When collaboration and communication need to be improved, office walls are the last place to look for a solution. The main walls hindering communication and collaboration are in your culture and, first and foremost, your management culture. "Flexible" offices will not make a rigid company more flexible because that rigidity is the result of a wider company culture, and that culture is determined for the most part by the leadership culture. In comparison with the huge impact of leadership culture, office layout pales into insignificance.

Of course, individual brainworkers all have the big personal responsibility to do what they can to improve their own intellectual productivity by regularly disconnecting from the internet, by avoiding multitasking, by managing their stress well and by getting sufficient sleep. For them I have written "BrainChains[5]" and the concise version "How to Unchain Your Brain[6]". The book covers the four BrainChains that they are personally responsible for. The Fifth BrainChain of open offices, in contrast, is predominantly the responsibility of managers and especially the executives.

---

5 Translated in Dutch, Russian and Chinese: see **www.brainchains.info**
6 Translated in Dutch and French: see **www.brainchains.info**

APPENDIX 1:
Why research and a book about "BrainChains"?

The trigger for writing "BrainChains" were "my" managers and professionals

The trigger for writing "BrainChains" were the challenges and questions of the many managers, executives and professionals in my lectures as well as training, coaching and consulting sessions, who were unknowingly ruining their intellectual productivity by the way they used our great IT technologies.

Given their interest, I added the subject to my talks, teaching and training about stress management, which is one of my core businesses. That hit the bull's-eye. The interest as well as the appreciation was awesome. Since so many participants wanted to read more about the subject I decided to postpone writing the book I had already started on Corporate Brain Disorder in order to write this one first.

A research-based book that is simple to read but not simplistic

I ended up screening more than 600 scientific publications and studying about 400. Here I have the advantage that I am a medical doctor, a neuropsychiatrist and a psychotherapist and that I have spent the greater part of my career in universities.

This allows me to understand a wide range of articles on subjects like neurology, physiology and (socio)psychology.

Moreover, I have spent the other part of my career as a consultant and trainer for a large variety of companies and organizations. This helps me to understand the reality of the office and the shop floor and to be practical in my advice.

Then it became my task to translate all the scientific jargon into terms that are easy to understand for lay people. I often burned the midnight oil to summarize all that information in a simple readable way.

A book full of practical tips, but before you change anything I'd first like you to really understand the issues

The second challenge was to let readers understand the issues so well that they can then find and develop their own creative solutions.

At the start I preferred not to give practical solutions but to let the readers invent their own based on the knowledge they gained. On the other hand, in my workshops I learned from the participants that they wanted examples of other people. Hence, since you can also learn by doing, or learn from other people's tricks, especially when you understand the basics, I added a practical section.

Therefore my book is divided into three parts. The first section explains how our brain works and why we should protect our thinking-brain. In the second section of "Brain-Chains" I explain how we unknowingly chain our brain. I clarify the "what" and the "why" and invite you to think about "how" you can apply the ideas to your own situation. In the third section, "How to unchain your brain", I describe lots of practical tips and tricks that have already helped other people, not necessarily for you to copy but to inspire you to find your own creative custom-made solutions.

Warning: the third challenge is yours: simple is not easy.

Easy to read and easy to understand does not mean easy to apply. Very simple advice can be very difficult to apply. However, if you do follow through, an increase of your intellectual productivity, creativity and a better stress-balance are guaranteed.

APPENDIX 2:
References

1   The Physical Environment of the Office: Contemporary and Emerging
    Issues. 2011 Matthew C. Davis
    International Review of Industrial and Organizational Psychology 2011

2   Hans Christian Andersen "Kejserens nye Klæder" 1837. Adapted from
    summaries: http://en.wikipedia.org/wiki/The_Emperor's_New_Clothes
    and http://shortstoriesshort.com/story/the-emperors-new-clothes/

3   Http://En.Wikipedia.Org/Wiki/Knowledge_Worker#Cite_Note-
    Davenport2005-1

4   The impact of the 'open' workspace on human collaboration. 2018
    Bernstein ES, Turban S. Phil.Trans.R.Soc.B 373: 20170239. http://dx.doi.
    org/10.1098/rstb.2017.0239

5   http://www.Businessweek.Com/Articles/2013-07-01/Ending-The-
    Tyranny-Of-The-Open-Plan-Office

6   Otterbring, T., Pareigis, J., Wästlund, E., Makrygiannis, A., & Lindström, A.
    (2018). The relationship between office type and job satisfaction: Testing
    a multiple mediation model through ease of interaction and well-being.
    Scandinavian journal of work, environment & health, 44(3), 330-334.

7   Richardson, A., Potter, J., Paterson, M., Harding, T., Tyler-Merrick,
    G., Kirk, R., ... & McChesney, J. (2017). Office design and health: A
    systematic review. Ann Richardson, 130(1467).

8   Al Horr Y, Arif M, Kaushik A, et al. Occupant productivity and office indoor
    environment quality: a review of the literature. Building and Environment.
    2016; 105:369–389.

9   De Croon, E., Sluiter, J., Kuijer, P. P., & Frings-Dresen, M. (2005). The
    effect of office concepts on worker health and performance: a systematic
    review of the literature. Ergonomics, 48(2), 119-134.

10 Kaarlela-Tuomaala, A., Helenius, R., Keskinen, E., & Hongisto, V. (2009).
    Effects of acoustic environment on work in private office rooms and open-
    plan offices–longitudinal study during relocation. Ergonomics, 52(11),
    1423-1444.

11 Bernstein, E. S., & Turban, S. (2018). The impact of the 'open'workspace
    on human collaboration. Phil. Trans. R. Soc. B, 373(1753), 20170239.

12 Kim, J., & De Dear, R. (2013). Workspace satisfaction: The privacy-
    communication trade-off in open-plan offices. Journal of Environmental
    Psychology, 36, 18-26.

13 Pejtersen, J. H., Feveile, H., Christensen, K. B., & Burr, H. (2011). Sickness absence associated with shared and open-plan offices—a national cross sectional questionnaire survey. Scandinavian journal of work, environment & health, 376-382.

14 Brennan, A., Chugh, J. S., & Kline, T. (2002). Traditional versus open office design: A longitudinal field study. Environment and behavior, 34(3), 279-299.

15 Charles, K. E., & Veitch, J. A. (2002). Environmental satisfaction in open-plan environments: 2. Effects of workstation size, partition height and windows. Institute for Reserch in Construction. National Reserch Council Canadá. Internal Report No. IRC-IR-845 (http://irc. nrccnrc. gc. ca/ircpubs), 21(03), 2007.

16 Oommen, V. G., Knowles, M., & Zhao, I. (2008). Should health service managers embrace open plan work environments?: A review. Asia Pacific Journal of Health Management, 3(2), 37.

17 Värlander, S. (2012). Individual flexibility in the workplace: A spatial perspective. The journal of applied behavioral science, 48(1), 33-61.

18 Wargocki, P., Frontczak, M., Schiavon, S., Goins, J., Arens, E., & Zhang, H. (2012). Satisfaction and self-estimated performance in relation to indoor environmental parameters and building features.

19 Smith-Jackson, T. L., & Klein, K. W. (2009). Open-plan offices: Task performance and mental workload. Journal of Environmental Psychology, 29(2), 279-289.

20 For A Summary: Stress: Friend And Foe. Theo Compernolle. Synergo. Order Www.Compernolle.Com TAB: Books and tools.

Workplace Air-Conditioning And Health Services Attendance Among French Middle-Aged Women: A Prospective Cohort Study. P Preziosi,S Czernichow, P Gehanno And S Hercberg. International Journal Of Epidemiology Volume 33, Issue 5 2004. Pp. 1120-1123.

Risk Factors In Heating, Ventilating, And Air-Conditioning Systems For Occupant Symptoms In US Office Buildings: The US EPA BASE Study. M. J. Mendell, Q.Lei-Gomez, A. G. Mirer, O.Seppänen,G. Brunner. Indoor Air. Volume 18, Issue 4, Pages 301–316, August 2008

21 Stress: Friend And Foe. Theo Compernolle.

22 Open-Plan Office Density And Environmental Satisfaction. Duval, C. L.; Charles, K. E.; Veitch, J. A. NRC Institute For Research In Construction; National Research Council Canada

Http://Www.Nrc-Cnrc.Gc.Ca/Obj/Irc/Doc/Pubs/Rr/Rr150/Rr150.Pdf

23 The impact of the 'open' workspace on human collaboration. 2018 Bernstein ES, Turban S. Phil.Trans.R.Soc.B 373: 20170239. http://dx.doi.org/10.1098/rstb.2017.0239

24 Office Type In Relation To Health, Well-Being, And Job Satisfaction Among Employees.

Christina Bodin Danielsson And Lennart Bodin,Environment And Behavior 2008 40: 636

Also: Http://Eab.Sagepub.Com/Content/40/5/636

25 Difference In Satisfaction With Office Environment Among Employees In Different Office Types. C Bodin Danielsson, L Bodin. Journal Of Architectural And Planning Research,Volume:26. Pages:241-257

See Among Many Others: The Physical Environment Of The Office: Contemporary And Emerging Issues. Matthew C. Davis, Desmond J. Leach, And Chris W. Clegg. International Review Of Industrial And Organizational Psychology, 2011, Volume 26,November 29, 2010. Chapter 6.P193

The Effect Of Office Concepts On Worker Health And Performance: A Systematic Review Of The Literature. Einar De Croona, Judith Sluitera, P Paul Kuijera & Monique Frings-Dresena

Ergonomics. Volume 48, Issue 2, 2005,Pages 119-134

Workspace Satisfaction: The Privacy-Communication Trade-Off In Open-Plan Offices, Jungsoo Kim, Richard De Dear, Journal Of Environmental Psychology, Volume 36, December 2013, Pages 18-26,

The Physical Environment Of The Office: Contemporary And Emerging Issues

Matthew C. Davis, Desmond J. Leach, And Chris W. Clegg

International Review Of Industrial And Organizational Psychology, 2011, Volume 26,November 29, 2010. Chapter 6.P193

26 Http://Www.Therichest.Com/Celebnetworth/Celebrity-Business/Tech-Millionaire/Scott-Adams-Net-Worth/

27 Thinking Outside The Cube. Jeffrey Pfeffer. Fortune May 14, 2007 Page B-8.

28 How To Create A Workplace People Never Want To Leave, Christopher Coleman. Bloomberg Businessweek. April 11, 2013

Http://Www.Businessweek.Com/Articles/2013-04-11/How-To-Create-A-Workplace-People-Never-Want-To-Leave-By-Googles-Christopher-Coleman#R=Lr-Fst

29 Should Health Service Managers Embrace Open Plan Work Environments? Vinesh G. Oommen, Mike Knowles, Isabella Zhao. A Review Asia Pacific Journal Of Health Management, Vol. 3, No. 2. (December 2008), Pp. 37-43

Workspace Satisfaction: The Privacy-Communication Trade-Off In Open-Plan Offices, Jungsoo Kim, Richard De Dear, Journal Of Environmental Psychology, Volume 36, December 2013, Pages 18-26,

Privacy And Communication In An Open-Plan Office. A Case Study. Eric Sundstrom. R. Kring Herbert. Environment And Behavior May 1982 Vol. 14 No. 3 379-392

30 Exposure To Disturbing Noise And Risk Of Long-Term Sickness Absence Among Office Workers: A Prospective Analysis Of Register-Based Outcomes

Thomas Clausen Jesper Kristiansen •Jørgen Vinsløv Hansen •Jan Hyld Pejtersen •Hermann Burr. Int Arch Occup Environ Health. 2012

Http://Link.Springer.Com/Content/Pdf/10.1007%2Fs00420-012-0810-4.Pdf

Stress And Open-Office Noise. Evans, Gary W.; Johnson, Dana. Journal Of Applied Psychology, Vol 85(5), Oct 2000, 779-783

Evans GW, Johnson D. Human Response To Open Office Noise. In: Carter N, Job RFS (Eds) Proceedings Of The International Congress On Noise As A Public Health Problem, Vol. 1. Sydney: Noise Effects '98 Pty, 1998; 255–8

Human Response To Open Office Noise. Evans GW, Johnson D. In: Carter N, Job RFS (Eds) Proceedings Of The International Congress On Noise As A Public Health Problem, Vol. 1. Sydney: Noise Effects '98 Pty, 1998; 255–8

The Influence Of Stressors On Biochemical Reactions - A Review Of Present Scientific Findings With Noise, Christian Maschke, Tanja Rupp, Karl Hecht, Christian Maschke, International Journal Of Hygiene And Environmental Health, Volume 203, Issue 1, 2000, Pages 45-53,

31 Tonya L. Smith-Jackson, Katherine W. Klein, Open-Plan Offices: Task Performance And Mental Workload, Journal Of Environmental Psychology, Volume 29, Issue 2, June 2009, Pages 279-289

32 Arthur Schopenhauer: On Noise. 1851

Translation By T. Bailey Saunders. Http://Www.Noisehelp.Com/Schopenhauer-Quotes.Html

See Also Ttp://Www.Schopenhauervereinigung.Com/Articles/Arthur-Schopenhauer-On-Noise/

33 Open-Plan Offices: Task Performance And Mental Workload, Tonya L. Smith-Jackson, Katherine W. Klein, Journal Of Environmental Psychology, Volume 29, Issue 2, June 2009, Pages 279-289

34 Http://Www.Gensler.Com/Uploads/Documents/2013_US_Workplace_ Survey_07_15_2013.Pdf

35 Why Do I Keep Interrupting Myself?: Environment, Habit And Self-Interruption. Laura Dabbish, Victor M. Gonzále, Gloria Mark. Proceedings Of The 2011 Annual Conference On Human Factors In Computing Systems. ACM New York, NY, USA ©2011

36 Http://Www.Gensler.Com/Uploads/Documents/2013_US_Workplace_ Survey_07_15_2013.Pdf

37 Arthur Schopenhauer: On Noise. 1851 Translation By T. Bailey Saunders. Ttp://Www.Schopenhauervereinigung.Com/Articles/Arthur-Schopenhauer-On-Noise/ Also At Http://Www.Noisehelp.Com/Schopenhauer-Quotes. Html

38 The Effect Of Sound On Office Productivity. CM Mak. YP Lui. BUILDING SERV ENG RES TECHNOL August 2012 Vol. 33 No. 3 339-345

A 3 Year Update On The Influence Of Noise On Performance And Behavior. Clark C, Sörqvist P. Noise Health 2012;14:292-6

Http://Www.Noiseandhealth.Org/Text.Asp?2012/14/61/292/104896

Open-Plan Office Noise: Cognitive Performance And Restoration, Helena Jahncke, Staffan Hygge, Niklas Halin, Anne Marie Green, Kenth Dimberg, Journal Of Environmental Psychology, Volume 31, Issue 4, December 2011, Pages 373-382

Perception And Evaluation Of Noise Sources In Open Plan Office. Marjorie Pierrette, Etienne Parizet, And Patrick Chevret. POMA Volume 19, Pp. 040127 (June 2013); Http://Scitation.Aip.Org/Getpdf/Servlet/Getpdfservle t?Filetype=Pdf&Id=PMARCW000019000001040127000001&Idtype=Cvi ps&Doi=10.1121/1.4800003&Prog=Normal

A Model Of Satisfaction With Open-Plan Office Conditions: COPE Field Findings. Jennifer A. Veitch Kate E. Charles,Kelly M.J. Farley And Guy R. Newshama. Journal Of Environmental Psychology. Volume 27, Issue 3, September 2007, Pages 177-189. Also At: Http://Www.Nrc-Cnrc.Gc.Ca/ Obj/Irc/Doc/Pubs/Nrcc49209/Nrcc49209.Pdf

Office Noise, Satisfaction, And Performance. Eric Sundstrom, Jerri P. Town, Robert W. Rice, David P. Osborn,Michael Brill. Environment And Behavior March 1994 Vol. 26 No. 2 195-222.

A Study On 2,391 Employees At 58 Sites.

Workspace Satisfaction: The Privacy-Communication Trade-Off In Open-Plan Offices, Jungsoo Kim, Richard De Dear, Journal Of Environmental Psychology, Volume 36, December 2013, Pages 18-26,

Making The Open-Plan Office A Better Place To Work. G.R. Newsham. Construction Technology Update No. 60, Dec. 2003

Perception And Evaluation Of Noise Sources In Open Plan Office. Marjorie Pierrette, Etienne Parizet, And Patrick Chevret. POMA Volume 19, Pp. 040127 (June 2013); Http://Scitation.Aip.Org/Getpdf/Servlet/Getpdfservlet?Filetype=Pdf&Id=PMARCW000019000001040127000001&Idtype=Cvips&Doi=10.1121/1.4800003&Prog=Normal

Work Performance And Mental Workload In Multiple Talker Environments. Ange Ebissou, Patrick Chevret, And Etienne Parizet. POMA Volume 19, Pp. 040128 (June 2013)

A Model Predicting The Effect Of Speech Of Varying Intelligibility On Work Performance. Hongisto, V. (2005), Indoor Air, 15: 458–468.

39 Open-Plan Office Noise: Cognitive Performance And Restoration, Helena Jahncke, Staffan Hygge, Niklas Halin, Anne Marie Green, Kenth Dimberg, Journal Of Environmental Psychology, Volume 31, Issue 4, December 2011, Pages 373-382

Mental arithmetic and non-speech office noise: An exploration of interference-by-content. Perham Nick, Hodgetts Helen, Banbury Simon. 2013 Volume: 15 62 Page: 73-78

40 Effects Of Noise On The Performance Of Rats In An Operant Discrimination Task.

J.H.R Maesa And G De Groot; Behavioural Processes; Volume 61, Issues 1–2, 28 February 2003, Pages 57–68

41 Jason Smucny, Donald C. Rojas, Lindsay C. Eichman, Jason R. Tregellas, Neuronal Effects Of Auditory Distraction On Visual Attention, Brain And Cognition, Volume 81, Issue 2, March 2013, Pages 263-270

42 Noise, psychosocial stress and their interaction in the workplace, Phil Leather, Diane Beale, Lucy Sullivan, Journal of Environmental Psychology, Volume 23, Issue 2, June 2003, Pages 213-222

Evaluations of effects due to low-frequency noise in a low demanding work situation, J. Bengtsson, K. Persson Waye, A. Kjellberg, Journal of Sound and Vibration, Volume 278, Issues 1–2, 22 November 2004, Pages 83-99

43 The Joint Effects Of Noise, Job Complexity, And Gender On Employee Sickness Absence: An Exploratory Study Across 21 Organizations — The CORDIS Study. Yitzhak Fried, Samuel Melamed, Haim A. Ben-David. Journal Of Occupational And Organizational Psychology. Volume 75, Issue 2, Pages 131–144, June 2002 ⊠ In White-Collar Workers

Health Effects Caused By Noise : Evidence In The Literature From The Past 25 Years. Ising H, Kruppa B. Noise Health 2004 Aug 29;6:5-13. Http://Www.Noiseandhealth.Org/Text.Asp?2004/6/22/5/31678

Stress Reactions To Cognitively Demanding Tasks And Open-Plan Office Noise. Jesper Kristiansen, Line Mathiesen, Pernille Kofoed Nielsen, Åse Marie Hansen, Hitomi Shibuya, Helga Munch Petersen, Søren Peter Lund, Jørgen Skotte, Marie Birk Jørgensen And Karen Søgaard. International Archives Of Occupational And Environmental Health. Volume 82, Number 5, 2009, P631-641.

Occupational Exposure To Noise And The Cardiovascular System: A Meta-Analysis, G. Tomei, M. Fioravanti, D. Cerratti, A. Sancini, E. Tomao, M.V. Rosati, D. Vacca, T. Palitti, M. Di Famiani, R. Giubilati, S. De Sio, F. Tomei, Science Of The Total Environment, Volume 408, Issue 4, 15 January 2010, Pages 681-689

W. Babisch, H. Ising, J.E.J. Gallacher, P.C. Elwood, P.M. Sweetnam, J.W.G. Yarnell, D. Bainton, I.A. Baker, Traffic Noise, Work Noise And Cardiovascular Risk Factors: The Caerphilly And Speedwell Collaborative Heart Disease Studies, Environment International, Volume 16, Issues 4–6, 1990, Pages 425-435

Physiological Aspects Of Noise-Induced Stress And Annoyance. R. Rylander. Journal Of Sound And Vibration. Volume 277, Issue 3, 22 October 2004, Pages 471-478

Noise Exposure And Public Health. Willy Passchier-Vermeer And Wim F. Passchier. Environmental Health Perspectives *Vol 108, Supplement 1 * March 2000. Http.//Ehpnetl.Niehs.Nih.Gov/Docs/2000/Suppl-1/123-131passchier-Vermeer/Abstract.Html

Http://Www.Ncbi.Nlm.Nih.Gov/Pmc/Articles/PMC1637786/Pdf/ Envhper00310-0128.Pdf

Health Effects Caused By Noise : Evidence In The Literature From The Past 25 Years. Ising H, Kruppa B. Noise Health 2004 Aug 29;6:5-13. Http://Www.Noiseandhealth.Org/Text.Asp?2004/6/22/5/31678

Stress Reactions To Cognitively Demanding Tasks And Open-Plan Office Noise. Jesper Kristiansen, Line Mathiesen, Pernille Kofoed Nielsen, Åse Marie Hansen, Hitomi Shibuya, Helga Munch Petersen, Søren Peter Lund, Jørgen Skotte, Marie Birk Jørgensen And Karen Søgaard. International Archives Of Occupational And Environmental Health. Volume 82, Number 5, 2009, P631-641.

Low Frequency Noise Enhances Cortisol Among Noise Sensitive Subjects During Work Performance. Kerstin Persson Waye, Johanna Bengtsson, Ragnar Rylander, Frank Hucklebridge, Phil Evans, Angela Clow. Life Sci. 2002 Jan 4;70 (7):745-58

Emotion And Meaning In Interpretation Of Sound Sources. Bergman, Penny; Vastfjall, Daniel; Fransson, Niklas; Sköld, Anders. The Journal Of The Acoustical Society Of America, Vol. 123, Issue 5, P. 3567

Physiological Aspects Of Noise-Induced Stress And Annoyance. R. Rylander. Journal Of Sound And Vibration. Volume 277, Issue 3, 22 October 2004, Pages 471-478

Urinary And Salivary Stress Hormone Levels While Performing Arithmetic Calculation In A Noisy Environment. Miki K, Kawamorita K, Araga Y, Musha T, Sudo A. Ind Health 1998;36:66-9

Noise Exposure And Public Health. Willy Passchier-Vermeer And Wim F. Passchier. Environmental Health Perspectives *Vol 108, Supplement 1 * March 2000. Http.//Ehpnetl.Niehs.Nih.Gov/Docs/2000/Suppl-1/123-131passchier-Vermeer/Abstract.Html

Http://Www.Ncbi.Nlm.Nih.Gov/Pmc/Articles/PMC1637786/Pdf/Envhper00310-0128.Pdf

44 Low Frequency Noise Enhances Cortisol Among Noise Sensitive Subjects During Work Performance,

Kerstin Persson Waye, Johanna Bengtsson, Ragnar Rylander, Frank Hucklebridge, Phil Evans, Angela Clow, Life Sciences, Volume 70, Issue 7, 4 January 2002, Pages 745-758

45 Stress And Open-Office Noise. Evans, Gary W.; Johnson, Dana. Journal Of Applied Psychology, Vol 85(5), Oct 2000, 779-783.

46 Effects Of Classroom Acoustics And Self-Reported Noise Exposure On Teachers' Well-Being. Jesper Kristiansen Roger Persson Søren Peter Lund Hitomi Shibuya Per Møberg Nielsen . Environment And Behavior February 2013 Vol. 45 No. 2 283-300

47 Arthur Schopenhauer: On Noise. 1851 Translation By T. Bailey Saunders. Ttp://Www.Schopenhauervereinigung.Com/Articles/Arthur-Schopenhauer-On-Noise/ Also At http://www.Noisehelp.Com/Schopenhauer-Quotes.Html

48 Stress: Friend And Foe. Theo Compernolle. Synergo 1999 / Lannoo 2011

49 A Model Predicting The Effect Of Speech Of Varying Intelligibility On Work Performance. Hongisto, V. (2005), Indoor Air, 15: 458–468.

50 Effects On Performance And Work Quality Due To Low Frequency Ventilation Noise, K. Persson Waye, R. Rylander, S. Benton, H.G. Leventhall, Journal Of Sound And Vibration, Volume 205, Issue 4, 28 August 1997, Pages 467-474

51 Arthur Schopenhauer: On Noise. 1851 Translation By T. Bailey Saunders. Ttp://Www.Schopenhauervereinigung.Com/Articles/Arthur-Schopenhauer-On-Noise/ Also At Http://Www.Noisehelp.Com/Schopenhauer-Quotes. Html

52 Open-Plan Office Noise: The Susceptibility And Suitability Of Differentcognitive Tasks For Work In The Presence Of Irrelevant Speech

Helena Jahncke. Noise & Health (2012) In Http://Pure.Ltu.Se/Portal/ Files/40220521/Helena_Jahncke.Komplett.Pdf

Cognitive Performance During Irrelevant Speech: Effects Of Speech Intelligibility And Office-Task Characteristics

Helena Jahncke, Valtteri Hongisto, & Petra Virjonen. Applied Acoustics (2012) In Helena Jahncke. Noise & Health (2012) In Http://Pure.Ltu.Se/ Portal/Files/40220521/Helena_Jahncke.Komplett.Pdf

53 A Model Predicting The Effect Of Speech Of Varying Intelligibility On Work Performance. Hongisto, V. (2005), Indoor Air, 15: 458–468.

Work Performance And Mental Workload In Multiple Talker Environments. Ange Ebissou, Patrick Chevret, And Etienne Parizet. POMA Volume 19, Pp. 040128 (June 2013)

54 Emberson L And Goldstein M., "Overheard Cell-Phone Conversations: When Less Speech Is More Distracting," Psychological Science.

The Effect Of Speech And Speech Intelligibility On Task Performance. N. Venetjokia, A. Kaarlela-Tuomaalaa, E. Keskinenb & V. Hongistoa. Ergonomics. Volume 49, Issue 11, 2006

55 Effects Of Five Speech Masking Sounds On Performance And Acoustic Satisfaction. Implications For Open-Plan Offices. Haapakangas, A.; Kankkunen, E.; Hongisto, V.; Virjonen, P.; Oliva, D.; Keskinen, E. Acta Acustica United With Acustica, Volume 97, Number 4, July/August 2011 , Pp. 641-655(15)

We Have Created This Collection Of Photographs Mainly To Serve As An Easy To Access Educational Resource. Contact Curator@Old-Picture.Com

56 How To Create A Workplace People Never Want To Leave, Christopher Coleman. Bloomberg Businessweek. April 11, 2013

Http://Www.Businessweek.Com/Articles/2013-04-11/How-To-Create-A-Workplace-People-Never-Want-To-Leave-By-Googles-Christopher-Coleman#R=Lr-Fst

57 Links Between Occupant Complaint Handling And Building Performance. Goins, John And Moezzi, Mithra. 2012. Series:Indoor Environmental Quality Http://Escholarship.Org/Uc/Item/4dr55189

58 Heidi Rasila, Peggie Rothe, (2012) "A problem is a problem is a benefit? Generation Y perceptions of open-plan offices", Property Management, Vol. 30 Issue: 4, pp.362-375

59 Thinking Outside The Cube. Jeffrey Pfeffer. Fortune May 14, 2007 Page B-8.

60 https://mashable.com/2012/08/25/frank-gehry-facebook-hq/?europe=true#m3D0nYgqfsqu

61 https://www.linkedin.com/feed/update/urn:li:activi ty:6377624893164437504

62 Doing gender in the 'new office' 2018 Alison Hirst , Christina Schwabenland. Gender, work and organization Volume25, Pages 159-176

63 Physical Order Produces Healthy Choices, Generosity, and Conventionality, Whereas Disorder Produces Creativity, 2013. Kathleen D. Vohs, Joseph P. Redden, and Ryan Rahinel. Psychological Science . Vol 24, Issue 9, pp. 1860 - 1867

   The Messy Desk Effect: How Tidiness Affects the Perception of Others. 1984, Sarah Sitton. The Journal of Psychology. Volume 117, 1984 - Issue 2

   Diplomas, Photos, and Tchotchkes as Symbolic Self-Representations: Understanding Employees' Individual Use of Symbols. 2015 Kris Byron and Gregory A. Laurence, Academy of Management JournalVol. 58, No. 1

64 Http://Www.Studio-Kg.Com/Objects-Index/B045_Deskshell/13279453

65 Effects Of Five Speech Masking Sounds On Performance And Acoustic Satisfaction. Implications For Open-Plan Offices. Haapakangas, A.; Kankkunen, E.; Hongisto, V.; Virjonen, P.; Oliva, D.; Keskinen, E. Acta Acustica United With Acustica, Volume 97, Number 4, July/August 2011 , Pp. 641-655(15)

   We Have Created This Collection Of Photographs Mainly To Serve As An Easy To Access Educational Resource. Contact Curator@Old-Picture.Com

66 Mental Performance In Noise: The Role Of Introversion, G. Belojevic, V. Slepcevic, B. Jakovljevic, Journal Of Environmental Psychology, Volume 21, Issue 2, June 2001, Pages 209-213

   Music While You Work: The Differential Distraction of Background Music on the Cognitive Test Performance of Introverts and Extraverts. ADRIAN FURNHAM* and ANNA BRADLEY. Appl. Cognit. Psychol. 11: 445 (1997)

67 The Effect Of Background Music And Background Noise On The Task Performance Of Introverts And Extraverts

   G Cassidy... - Psychology Of Music, 2007 Sagepublications

Music Is As Distracting As Noise: The Differential Distraction Of Background Music And Noise On The Cognitive Test Performance Of Introverts And Extraverts; A Furnham, L Strbac - Ergonomics, 2002 - Taylor & Francis

Work Efficiency And Personality; A Comparison Of Introverted And Extraverted Subjects Exposed To Conditions Of Distraction And Distortion Of Stimulus In A Learning Task; F. S. Morgensterna, R. J. Hodgsonb & L. LA; Ergonomics Volume 17, Issue 2, 1974 - Taylor & Francis

68 Succesgids Voor Families Met Een Bedrijf. Theo Compernolle. Lanno/ Synergo. 2002

69 Excellent Practical Ideas And Solutions Can Be Found In The In Depth Research Instigated By The National Research Council Canada: Cost-Effective Open-Plan Environments (COPE) A Team Of Psychologists, Physicists, Architects, And Engineers Did Experiments And Field Studies. They Provide Excellent Reports And Tools To Analyse The Office Environment

70 Senses, Brain and Spaces Workshop. Peter Barrett, Lucinda Barrett. The Think Lab, University of Salford. March 8th and 9th 2007 http://usir. salford.ac.uk/19507/1/FINAL_SBS_WORKSHOP_REPORT.pdf

The effects of window proximity, partition height, and gender on perceptions of open-plan offices, Journal of Environmental Psychology, Volume 27, Issue 2, June 2007, Pages 154-165, http://www. sciencedirect.com/science/article/pii/S0272494407000059

Daylight for Energy Savings and Psycho-Physiological Well-Being in Sustainable Built Environments. Sergio Altomonte. Journal of Sustainable Development 2008. Vol. 1, No. 3

More feedback from readers of BrainChains

Excellent Book. I was addicted to "multitasking" and had trouble concentrating in longer tasks... Can honestly say that this book has changed me for the better! It is written in a very readable fashion and contains practical tips on how to make you brain work better and more efficiently. It's a kind of "User manual to your brain". How to use it correctly to gain the most stress free productivity...

Jose Rivero

Being filled all the time by all kinds of electronic information every day, I often feel myself lost in this "ICT world". How can we live and what shall we live as human? This book shows me a so powerful human brain ... Looking inside into my brain, I get my idea to have my life back under my own control, just like what is said in the last poem: Recapture time to love and be loved, it is the keystone of happiness and resilience: yours and theirs.

Wei TAO, Business Information Manager

Wow. 6/12 into purchase of this book is still being pulled on and off my shelf. An amazing insight into our brain-possibly the best computer we will ever have the pleasure of owning! I've Learned lots already from this entertaining academic. Enlightening.

S.A.W. Bristol UK

Brilliant book and explodes all the rubbishy myths about multitasking

10HS

... blending his best knowledge in medical sciences and leadership development to give us a real eye opener on how our brain is working (or not) in our new environment.

Serge Zimmerlin. Group Vice President

The book was a revelation for me and helped me better understand why people do what they do in a health & safety context. An essential and easy read for practical people, who want to know how people work and what can be practically done to maximize their efficiency and reduce human error"

Malc Staves Global Health & Safety Director

... Innovations that work are selected and thrive, but some, like IT and hyperconnectedness, overshoot and threaten to become runaway phenomena. It took Prof. Compernolle's unique synthesis of brain science, expertise in human behavior and therapeutical skills to also provide remedies and to progress from Drucker's 'knowledge work' to Compernolle's 'brainwork'.

Prof. Jan Bernheim

A MUST READ for managers overall, but especially for responsible HR managers as the productivity of esp. white-collar employees is truly at risk in the 'Anytime, Anyplace' connected world of today. The research and in-practice evidence is overwhelming why we should not multitask, always be connected or take short cuts on our sleep. I compare the impact of this book to the "Shallows: what the internet does to our brains" by N.Carr.

I have changed my personal habits immediately and now also inspire people around me at work and in my private life to do the same.

Philippe

It's obvious that our best tool to work and live it's our brain but unfortunately we often forget the way to use it correctly. Theo, in the funniest way I know, has found the right way to open my mind and improve my daily performance. Reading this book you will know how many mistakes make every day avoiding to use our brain correctly and how much time/money we could save hearing our body signals.

Ferdinand

"...Multitasking is impossible! Understanding and accepting this, helped me to refocus on tasks which matters and to rediscover my creativity. I used the short MULTITASKING test in my meetings in our global organization. It's exciting to see everywhere the "aha"-effect, the epiphany!"

Dr. Peter zum Hebel, Vice President

An absolute must if we want to safeguard or recover our brain's full capacity, productivity and creativity. A wise lesson to better master the ever growing number of addictive ICT-tools, thus improving our quality of life both at home and at work, and, who knows, even saving lives. And finally, a plea for more direct and true relationships in the real world instead of losing precious time in a mostly shallow virtual world

Prof Gino Baron

This book provides a number of important data that caution us to ask ourselves important questions about our habits and how we ruin our companies, families, health and safety by blindly following manufacturers of various gadgets. Highly recommended!

Vedran Vucic